BOUNDARIES OF HOME:

MAPPING FOR LOCAL EMPOWERMENT

Edited by
DOUG ABERLEY

THE NEW CATALYST BIOREGIONAL SERIES

NEW SOCIETY PUBLISHERS

Gabriola Island, BC   Philadelphia, PA

Canadian Cataloguing in Publication Data

Main entry under title:

Boundaries of home

(*The New Catalyst* Bioregional Series; 6)
Includes bibliographical references.
ISBN 1-55092-206-8 (bound). -- ISBN 1-55092-207-6 (pbk.)

1. Environmental mapping. 2. Landscape changes -- Maps.
3. Human ecology. 4. Cartography. I. Aberley, Doug. II. Series.
GF23.C35B68 1993   304.2'3   C93-091503-8

Inquiries regarding requests to reprint all or part of *Boundaries of Home: Mapping for Local Empowerment* should be addressed to:
  New Society Publishers,
  P.O.Box 189, Gabriola Island BC, Canada V0R 1X0,
or
  4527 Springfield Avenue, Philadelphia PA, U.S.A. 19143.

Canada ISBN: 1-55092-207-6 (Paperback)
Canada ISBN: 1-55092-206-8 (Hardback)
USA ISBN: 0-86571-272-7 (Paperback)
USA ISBN: 0-86571-271-9 (Hardback)

Cover design by David Lester from the map, "Landforms of North America," by Erwin Raisz.

Printed in Canada on partially recycled paper by Hignell Printing Limited, Winnipeg, Manitoba.

To order directly from the publishers, please add $2.50 to the price for the first copy, 75 cents each additional copy (plus GST in Canada). Send check or money order to:
  New Society Publishers,
  P.O.Box 189, Gabriola Island, BC V0R 1X0, Canada,
or
  4527 Springfield Avenue, Philadelphia, PA 19143, U.S.A.

New Society Publishers is a project of the New Society Educational Foundation, a non-profit, tax-exempt public foundation in the U.S. and the Catalyst Education Society, a non-profit educational society in Canada. Opinions expressed in this book do not necessarily reflect positions of the New Society Educational Foundation, nor the Catalyst Education Society.

Boundaries of Home is the sixth of *The New Catalyst*'s Bioregional Series which is also available by subscription. Write: P.O. Box 189, Gabriola Island, BC V0R 1X0, Canada.

The New Catalyst Bioregional Series

*T*he New Catalyst Bioregional Series was begun in 1990, the start of what some were calling "the turnaround decade" in recognition of the warning that humankind had ten years to turn around its present course, or risk such permanent damage to planet Earth that human life would likely become unviable. Unwilling to throw in the towel, *The New Catalyst's* editorial collective took up the challenge of presenting, in new form, ideas and experiences that might radically influence the future.

As a tabloid, *The New Catalyst* magazine has been published quarterly since 1985. From the beginning, an important aim was to act as a catalyst among the diverse strands of the alternative movement—to break through the overly sharp dividing lines between environmentalists and aboriginal nations; peace activists and permaculturalists; feminists, food co-ops, city-reinhabitants and back-to-the-landers—to promote healthy dialogue among all these tendencies working for progressive change, for a new world. The emerging bioregional movement was itself a catalyst and umbrella for these groups, and so *The New Catalyst* became a bioregional journal for the northwest, consciously attempting to draw together the local efforts of people engaged in both resistance and renewal from as far apart as northern British Columbia, the Great Lakes, and the Ozark mountains, as well as the broader, more global thinking of key people from elsewhere in North America and around the world.

To broaden its readership, *The New Catalyst* changed format, the tabloid reorganized to include primarily material of regional importance, and distributed free, and the more enduring articles of relevance to a wider, continental audience now published twice yearly in *The New Catalyst's* Bioregional Series—a magazine in book form! Through this new medium, we hope to encourage on-going dialogue among overlapping networks of interest, to solidify our common ground, expand horizons, and provoke deeper analysis of our collective predicament as well as a sharing of those practical, local initiatives that are the cutting edge of more widespread change.

The Bioregional Series aims to inspire and stimulate the building of new, ecologically sustainable cultures and communities in their myriad facets through presenting a broad spectrum of concerns ranging from how we view the world and act within it, through efforts at restoring damaged ecosystems or greening the cities, to the raising of a new and hopeful generation. It is designed not for those content with merely saving what's left, but for those forward-looking folk with abundant energy for life, upon whom the future of Earth depends.

Other volumes in the series include *Turtle Talk: Voices For A Sustainable Future,* (No.1), *Green Business: Hope or Hoax?* (No.2), *Putting Power In Its Place: Create Community Control!* (No.3), *Living With The Land: Communities Restoring The Earth* (No.4), and *Circles of Strength: Community Alternatives to Alienation* (No.5).

The *Bioregional Series* and *The New Catalyst* magazine are available at a discount by subscription. Write for details to: *The New Catalyst,* P.O. Box 189, Gabriola Island, B.C., Canada V0R 1X0.

Table of Contents

Acknowledgments

This book is the collective work of many people who share an equal dedication to maps and the sense of place they can evoke. All contributors freely donated their writing in the hope that cartography and the bioregional vision would be better understood as a powerful tool of empowerment. Their assistance is appreciated beyond measure.

There are others I would like to thank for their contribution to seeing this work into print. Chris Plant patiently helped to suggest and evolve the contents of this book, while New Society Publishers in general approved support of a rather different type of volume than usual. Tony Pearse, Ken Hoke, Henry Lipsett, and Dr. JeremyRaemaekers assisted with references. And, finally, thanks to Amandah, Christine, and Megan who have lived for months with maps everywhere.

Mapping is a deceptively complex topic that has been more difficult to describe than anticipated. As I have tried to weave many disparate pieces together into a whole, responsibility for errors or omissions is mine.

Grateful acknowledgment is also made for permission to reprint previously published articles from the following sources:

"Mapping Your Roots: Parish Mapping," by Angela King is reprinted with permission of the author from *Geographical Magazine*, May 1991, pages 40-43.

"GIS in Friends of the Earth, U.K.: 1990s Technology Meets 1990s Needs," by Jonathan Doig is reprinted with permission of the author from *Mapping Awareness and GIS in Europe*, Vol. 6, No. 4 (May 1992), pp.9-12.

"Four Reasons Why You've Never Seen a Map of the Northern California Bioregion," by Seth Zuckerman is reprinted with permission of the author from *Upriver Downriver*, Issue 14 (1992), pp.8-9. Subscriptions are CAN$15.00 or US$10.00 from: P.O. Box 103, Petrolia, CA 95558, U.S.A.

"On Ecoregional Boundaries," by David McCloskey is reprinted with permission of the author from *Earth Ethics*, Summer 1992, pp.7-8.

"Wild At The Heart," by George Tukel is reprinted with permission of the author from *Upriver Downriver*, Issue 14 (1992), pp.10-14.

"Step One: Mapping The Biosphere," by Gene Marshall is a shortened version of the article, "Step One Toward a Sustainable Human Presence on Planet Earth: An Essay on Social Strategy," first published in *Realistic Living: A Journal of Ethics and Religion*, No. 17 (Nov. 1992), pp.2-6, and is reprinted with permission of the author. Subscriptions are US$10.00 from Rt.3, Box 104-A5, Bonham, TX 75418, U.S.A.

For illustration credits, thanks to the British Museum for permission to copy an image of a Marshall Island sea chart (Ref. 1904-6-21.34); the Kitimat-Stikine Regional District and Dr. Tom Richards for their map of the Hazelton area; David McCloskey for his image of Cascadia; and Paul Jance of the University of British Columbia for permission to use his "Pacific Northwest" base map. Illustrations in articles by Angela King, Seth Zuckerman, Kirkpatrick Sale, and George Tukel were kindly supplied by the authors. The remaining illustrations are the work of the editor.

This volume is dedicated to the future of Caledonia — old and new.

Doug Aberley
Edinburgh, Alba

1

The Lure of Mapping: An Introduction

Doug Aberley

If you gather a group of people together and ask them about maps you will always get a lively response. Like the universal fascination with moving water, or the dance of a fire's flame, maps hold some primal attraction for the human animal. For some, it is the memory of a treasure map followed in youth, or a scramble to a mountain vista etched forever in personal memory. For others, it is an almost magical chance to see what otherwise is hidden: the relationship of hill to forest to settlement to ruin. And, for yet others, maps unravel the mysteries of the present and future of place through the depiction of fixed and flowing energy layered in patterns of opportunity. Whether in our minds, or printed on paper, maps are powerful talismans that add form to our individual and social reality. They are models of the world — icons if you wish — for what our senses "see" through the filters of environment, culture, and experience.

When the fundamental importance of perceiving real and imagined space is compared to what passes for most mapping today, a huge separation is apparent. In our consumer society, mapping has become an activity primarily reserved for those in power, used to delineate the "property" of nation states and multinational companies. The making of maps has become dominated by specialists who wield satellites and other complex machinery. The result is that although we have great access to maps, we have also lost the ability ourselves to *conceptualize, make* and *use* images of place — skills which our ancestors honed over thousands of years. In return for this surrendered knowledge, maps have been appropriated for uses which are more and more sinister. Spewed forth from digital abstraction, they guide the incessant development

1

juggernaut. They divide whole local, regional and continental environments into the absurdity of squared efficiency. They aid in attaching legitimacy to a reductionist control that strips contact with the web of life from the experience of place.

The illusion persists that maps still play a vital part in our lives. There exist thousands of atlases, posters of Earth viewed from space, and books on cartographic minutiae. We see endless television flashes of maps showing the location of the latest war, or plane crash. Images of the planet lend credibility to the selling of insurance, pop drinks, and other "important" things. Maps have become popular investments to be hoarded, and under no circumstance used for any practical purpose. Yet amongst this avalanche of geographic blather, there are only two types of maps that most people really seem to use: the ubiquitous highway or tourist map that guides us ever onward to the next consumer experience; and the useful sterility of the topographic sheet which allows us mild adventure in the guise of tourism.

If you were entirely cynical, you could view the appropriation of mapping from common understanding as just another police action designed to assist the process of homogenizing 5,000 human cultures into one malleable and docile market. As a collective entity we have lost our languages, have forgotten our songs and legends, and now cannot even conceive of the space that makes up that most fundamental aspect of life — home.

Realization of this sad condition can breed two reactions. The first is to be defeated by forces which seem too powerful and amorphous to change. But this book is about an opposite response, an understanding that no imposed homogenization can succeed against those who wisely evolve culture and technology connected to the womb of all human endeavor — the flats and folds of thousands of niche ecosystems.

In direct opposition to the paradigm of the single global market, people are articulating a competing vision in a healthy variety of ways. Aboriginal peoples are courageously defending themselves against cultural and physical genocide. Societies swallowed in the last two hundred years of industrialization are awakening from a slumber imposed by promises of the nation state. And, perhaps most important, people of many origins who find themselves newly planted in city or in country are asserting their aspirations for political and economic regimes that mix the best of all their origins. In all three movements there is a joyful relearning of what has been taken, lost, or forgotten. At the same time, the ways of the past are being adapted to a present that offers challenging opportunities for the use of technologies which allow self-reliance and interdependence. The common element is that of reinhabitation — of place, of traditions old and new, of a future based on local aspirations for stability, quality of life, and interconnection.

Many movements and philosophies have tried to organize the indefatigable human will for positive social change into a coherent doctrine. There are reasons why they fail — physical defeat, false leaders, co-option by media or money, lazy disregard for lessons of the past. Aware of these lessons and pitfalls, the reinhabitant movement has been almost invisible as it spreads its quiet logic across continents. As befits the awkward confidence of this new path, it has chosen a name that does little to attract new adherents: "bioregionalism." This utilitarian mouthful of syllables conveys the task at hand — to wed dynamic human populations to distinct physical territories defined by continuities of land and life. The promise is that these bioregions will be inhabited in a manner that respects ecological carrying capacity, engenders social justice, uses appropriate technology creatively, and allows for a rich interconnection between regionalized cultures. This is no utopia; it is simply an evolution of the best of human society as it has been practiced over the millennia. Our bioregional future is based not on what has never been, but on that which is most familiar to our species.

Bioregionalists have been meeting in North America and Europe for nearly twenty years. We come from all walks of life and have typically evolved through a succession of activist movements organized around the achievement of civil rights, the end of war, the elimination of sexism and racism, and the protection of local and global environments. To place our activism in context we visited, and sometimes created, many philosophies — existentialism, social and deep ecology, Eastern and evangelical Christian religions, and more. Our search for alternatives led in scores of directions, the result often being individual growth on the one hand, but, on the other, the lack of even a loosely-conceived, shared purpose. For all our struggles, there remained a lack of some unifying vision that would tie all our efforts into some organic whole. The quest for this synthesis led to the origin of the bioregional ideal. It remains a delicate notion — rooted in tribal traditions, and able to adapt to the world of technology, limits, and interconnection. Bioregionalism is about bringing that which has been separated back together. We do not surrender affiliations to other causes, we simply share an understanding that our actions bear most fruit when interrelated in an ecologically- and culturally-defined place.

The purpose of this small volume is to describe the use of mapping as one of many tools bioregionalists can use in reinhabiting place. This is an ambitious assignment, but the type of challenge that must be met if we are to take our aspirations for social justice and ecosystem continuity beyond the realm of desire and philosophy into the terrain of empowerment and practice.

MAPS AS VISIONS

There are steps that all reinhabitants must take in the struggle to reclaim the commons. First, comes the perception that we are indeed living in a time of crisis, that the status quo must be reformed and ultimately replaced. Second, it is important to clearly understand the forces which subjugate land and life. Third, evolving a vision of the "new" reinhabitant culture is crucial. And fourth, the diverse talents of reinhabitants need to be loosely organized to both resist the intrinsic evil of the status quo, and concurrently to build the parallel reality of culture tied to finite and complex ecosystems. The goal of all this is not the imposition of some pre-ordained future, but a world where thousands of vital cultures can evolve within a spectrum of diversity bounded only by ecological limits and the right of all humans to enjoy social justice.

Mapping can play a useful role in all of these steps. The destruction of land and culture caused by big business and centralized government can be displayed visually with great effect. The wrong of clearcuts, suburbs on farmland, or toxic dumps which, in isolation, may seem unassociated, begin magically to communicate a larger evil when shown in graphic relationship. The cruel division of classes and the allocation of poverty based on race, sex, or age by the present political economy cannot be hidden when charted across our urban neighborhoods.

Maps can show a vision for the future more clearly than thousands of words. Cities envisioned as clusters of villages where the impacts of human concentration are offset by maximizing self-reliance and proper respect for supporting rural ecosystems; dispersed settlements interspaced in a web of wilderness and linked to sustainable sources of food and energy; or a community forest linked to a value-added sawmill, and powered by a hydro-electric plant that is located above restored salmon runs — such images begin to demonstrate the practical logic of the futures we see.

Maps can also depict strategies of resistance: where to block further unwise development, to identify landscapes that have been damaged, to describe alternatives to the incremental destruction of sustaining habitats. Urban development that fails to follow the laws of environmental protection can be shown via maps which focus knowledge of injustice into a persistent and powerful anger. Images that show how resistance is organized will likely make it easier for people in other regions to equally embrace the challenge of rooted defiance.

And images of place can make the actual building of an alternative a possibility. A bioregion-based culture will be grown in thousands of small and interrelated actions, the more coordinated in space and time, the better. Build a trail for access to a stream restoration project, extend it to take in a scenic vista of your valley region, construct a base camp for watershed guardians and outdoor education programs, use the trail to aid selective logging and wild food harvest. Chart patterns of urban creeksheds and open space, link them together, and use the emerging green web to define new villages whose stewards have more autonomy rather than more freeways as an agenda. Mapping, whether pencil- or computer-generated, becomes a graphic tool that allows the complexities of ecologically integrated societies to emerge in stable increments.

REDISCOVERING THE LANGUAGE OF TIME AND SPACE

It is one thing to agree that mapping can play an important role in social change, it is quite another to actually feel empowered to add mapping as a tool of everyday action. To nudge you to just such a confidence, here is some final advice — exhortations that even the most timid reinhabitant will not easily be able to ignore.

It is important to repeat over and over that there is no "good" mapping or "bad" mapping. Leave the need for perfection to the scientists; what you are being encouraged to do is honestly describe what you already know about where you live in a manner that adds momentum to positive forces of change. There is a learning curve that everyone goes through but, with experience, every region has the potential to be represented by as many unique interpretations as it has citizens. Reinhabitants will not only learn to put maps on paper, maps will also be sung, chanted, stitched and woven, told in stories, and danced across fire-lit skies.

No map shows reality perfectly. A map is an icon — a potent representation — but only a skeleton of what is real. The mistake of science is that its goal is to describe the world as a complex machine, and to replace the vagaries of nature's chaos with "management." Bioregional mapping is about something else: processes and relationships rather than disembodied facts. The notion that only experts can map is the type of disenfranchisement that reinhabitants confront and nullify. If it doesn't matter how well you draw, or that you have the "best" pens, or that you don't have a college degree in cartography, then what *does* matter? Simply the ability to try, to fill the world again with personal and communal descriptions of time and space.

Reinhabitants do not have to reinvent the craft of mapping. It is perfectly alright to use existing topographic, local government, or other maps of your home region as a fundamental resource. By sifting through maps that meticulously divide the world into pieces, and then layering this abstraction back into descriptions of whole ecosystems, you will spare yourself great energy and expense. Imagine the horror of government agencies who are inundated with people who want access to the knowledge their taxes have provided. And imagine if map-borne information generated for exploitation of land and life is redirected to an equally proficient quest for social justice and integration of human cultures with place!

It is also acceptable that not everyone will want to become absolutely skilled in the making of maps. But with no voice in the evolution of alternatives that maps can potently represent, images of the present industrial tyranny can easily be replaced with some different tyranny. So what *is* essential is that the *language* of describing time and space be regained so that we all can feel comfortable with a pencil in hand, tracing the aspirations that define self, family, and community. There will always be those among us who have an avocation to map, just as there are those who have a passion for dance or for welding. If we all become generalists, then at minimum we will possess the common language to contribute our vision to the images of bioregions that will emerge in more artistic form.

The final exhortation is the most important. Just *do* it! Go out and buy enough 1:50,000 scale (one mile to one inch) topographic maps so that the place where you live is in the center of a region of approximately 50 miles in diameter. Tape them together and use marking pens and colored pencils to highlight flows of water, changes in elevation, and the boundary of your neighborhood or small community. Buy some multicoloured adhesive "dots" and use different hues to show where you live, where your water comes from, and where your waste goes. In the map margins, note the dates of the hottest and coldest days, and list the birds and animals you see. In these many simple steps you begin to layer a customized understanding of part of a bioregion. Pin the map on your kitchen wall and marvel at the focus it will become for new insight and old debates. If entire communities were to embark on this "seeing" just think of the strength all the disparate perceptions could have when woven together!

Do you feel encouraged enough to wade in? The remainder of this book is organized to take you through a wide terrain of mapping lore.

Aboriginal mapping is evoked as inspiration. The experience of rein-habitants who are actually mapping in their home bioregions is de-scribed. A range of thought on current mapping issues follows. Step-by-step guidance is then given on a technique that can be used to identify and map your own bioregion. And, finally, an access section provides information on a wide range of additional mapping-related resources. Inspiration by example, inspiration by introduction to the frontiers of debate, the gift of a mapping primer — the next steps are up to you.

2

Eye Memory:
The Inspiration
of Aboriginal Mapping

Doug Aberley

Western society tends to be entirely preoccupied with the relatively narrow history and opinions of European culture. Unfortunately this chauvinism also holds true with most writing on mapping. In a number of volumes reviewed as sources for this chapter there is little mention of maps made by any other than those with European origins. There is a standard method to this exclusion. An initial chapter begins with the acknowldgement that aboriginal cultures used mapping, usually under the pejorative heading of the word "primitive." Several very scant examples are given, usually including pictures of the same two or three surviving cartographic specimens. In some volumes there is mention of Chinese and Islamic mapping, possibly because these sources mimicked the imperial goal shared by European colonizers. That's all! There then follow scores of pages elaborating in great detail how Greeks, Romans, Catalans, Dutch, English, and scientists in general have all pushed mapping technique and precision ever onward.

This volume breaks such tradition. Mapping as conceptualized and executed by aboriginal peoples is at the heart of what reinhabitants need to rediscover. How did societies that were rooted in place, that were wedded irrevocably to the land, use perceptions of time and space to provide order to their actions? Owing to the relentless subjugation of aboriginal cultures, it is difficult to find the answer to this fundamental question. Thankfully, there remain several paths of investigation available. This chapter looks at how aboriginal maps were physically made, how the environment was conceptualized, and then how contemporary

8

aboriginal cultures are using maps.

Before proceeding an important assumption should be made clear: all humans originate from aboriginal cultures. In all of us is some remnant of an ability to understand relationships of physical space to survival and the evolution of stable community life. In admiring the mapping of aboriginal cultures, the goal is not to copy others, but to rediscover in ourselves a genetic memory of ancient skills. This is no romantic quest. What we seek is inspiration from the best attributes of those who remain close to the land — rootedness, spirituality, and the ability to live in complex harmony with other life.

STICKS AND STONES

As just mentioned, most books on mapping give the same two or three examples of aboriginal maps. The most quoted example is of the sea-charts used by Micronesians living on the Marshall Islands in the north Pacific. Islanders construct these maps from pieces of the narrow center rib of a palm leaf tied together with coconut fiber. Grids are thus formed in distorted geometric patterns, depicting the curve, refraction, and intersection of wave patterns caused by prevailing winds. They tie shells to the frame to represent the location of islands. The sea-charts are made for differing uses. A *mattang* is made for instructional purposes, showing only examples of wave patterns that would be represented on a working sea-chart. A *meddo* depicts islands that form parts of larger archipelagos. A *rebbang* represents an entire island chain.

Usually only a physical description of this remarkable type of map is included in books on cartographic history. The fascinating cultural setting that has created the use of such images is left unexplained. Micronesians live on very small atolls scattered in four major clusters across a vast ocean — the Gilberts, Carolines, Marianas, and Marshalls. They face the frequent threat of devastating storms. They have needed, therefore, to devise reliable navigation techniques for moving humans to-and-fro for social purposes, for locating and harvesting resources, and for reciprocal trade. To accomplish these cultural goals, they faced two tasks. First, they had to invent a technology that enabled navigation across vast distances with the benefit of no typical landmarks; and, second, they needed a method of teaching that allowed this knowledge to be passed on. Each of these imperatives deserves further exploration.

How do you cross huge distances with no obvious physical guides? Oceans are a complex interaction of tides, currents and wind-driven wave patterns that are replicated in cycles over time. The steepness of waves, their pattern of refraction, or the amount of cresting can all

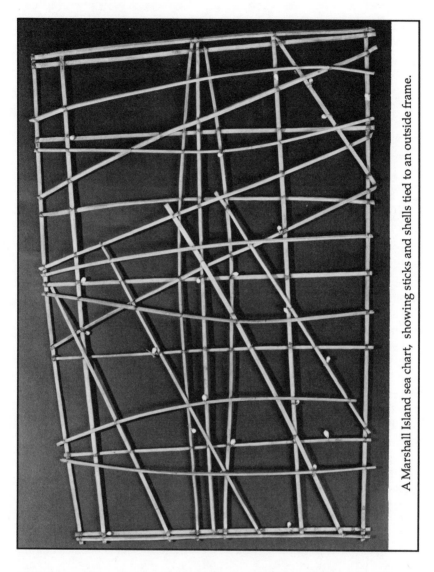

A Marshall Island sea chart, showing sticks and shells tied to an outside frame.

indicate location. Star configurations and their movement are markers that can be used with equal reliability. Species of birds that nest on land fly at a variety of distances from shore. Birds also fly at altitudes that make them visible to the human eye far more easily than a low atoll invisible over an unmarked horizon. Sea colors, sounds, water temperature, and phosphorescence change with depth, as do the type and variety of sea creatures that can be observed. Floating debris and smells travel in predictable patterns. Speed can be marked by the time a sail keeps a certain shape matched with the memory of how fast a particular canoe travelled in an equal breeze. Clouds form over land in a manner different from over the sea. This listing could go on at great length. The point is that people living "in place" have the ability to customize a worldview that allows the physical world to become alive with nuance and opportunity.

The way in which Micronesians teach this knowledge of time and space to succeeding generations is embedded deeply in their culture. Most Micronesians navigate, but they possess greatly differing levels of skill. Those invited to learn deeper levels of mapping skills are chosen for their aptitude or interest in the craft. Many are simply relatives of master navigators, steeped from early years in the complex mental mapping required. Micronesians pass on knowledge and the power it gives by a number of methods, all connected by the need to layer information in memory. Mapping lore is preserved verbally in stories, poems, chants, and through rhymes. It is shown physically in stick charts, in dwellings whose rafter patterns depict segments of the night sky, and in imaginary canoes surrounded by stones which mark tell-tales of distance and location. In these and many more ways, Micronesians weave information on navigation into their daily lives. The point is that mapping skills are not only for experts, and not just for scholarly reference; they are an everyday part of a society that is inextricably linked to its environment.

Books which provide a far more comprehensive description of Micronesian mapping include: *East is a Big Bird,* by Thomas Gladwin; *We the Navigators,* by David Lewis; and *A Song For Satawal,* by Kenneth Brower. A volume which relates Micronesian navigation to the concept of "knowledge as power" is *Unwritten Knowledge: A Case Study of the Navigators of Micronesia,* by Lyndsay Farrell.

PLANKS, BLOOD AND BARK

The second example most quoted is of the maps made by various tribes of Arctic Inuit. "Eskimos" of Kotzebue Sound near the Bering Strait would use beach sand and rocks to build scaled models of their territories. The map would be proportioned first by using a stick of random length to represent how far could be journeyed in a day. Based on this scale a coastline or interior landscape would be traced, with relief shown by mounded sand or piled stones. Sticks were placed upright in the sand to show locations used for fishing and other activities. When such maps were made there was much participation by those present. Greenland Inuit used driftwood planks to carve renditions of shoreline indentation and relief. These maps curved continuously around the plank, allowing the longest possible distance to be shown on the smallest map. The eloquence of this method is hard to fault. Travelling by kayak, what could be better than to have a waterproof guide that floated if dropped overboard?

There are only a very limited number of other sources of additional information on historic uses of mapping by traditional cultures. In 1910 a Russian cartographer by the name of B. F. Adler compiled a 350-page text titled *Karty Piervobytnyh Narodov* — "Maps of Primitive Peoples." This volume represents what is regarded as the best attempt to compile maps originating from aboriginal societies that were drawn prior to contact with European explorers. Adler assembled fifty-five maps from Asia, fifteen from the Americas, three from Africa, forty from Australia, and two from the East Indies. Although this volume is rare, and written in Russian, it was partially translated by H. De Hutorowicz for review in a 1911 edition of *Bulletin of the American Geographical Society*. It is from this source that the following additional examples of pre-industrial mapping are noted.

Tchuktchi (Siberia) people made maps drawn in reindeer blood on wood planks. These maps were illustrated with scenes of hunting, fishing and village life. Splashes of blood were used to show the elevation of hills. Another Siberian people, the Tungus, drew maps on birch bark. The information on their maps was not oriented to "north" or "south," but to the direction of flow of the dominant river artery. Aztecs made extremely accurate maps of their territory that were painted on a variety of materials, including fabric woven from agave fibre, skins, and fig bark paper. Because of the destruction ordered by Spanish military leaders, there are only two examples of this type of map still in existence. Maps from Africa, North and South America were traced on bark, skin, and bone, usually with water and shoreline as the central orientation.

In addition, there were many other methods aboriginal people used to bound and navigate their territories. Stone cairns, carved trees, painted rocks, and natural landmarks guided movement or identified places of particular interest or use. This marking of the physical world made the whole of a tribal territory a map, a complex pattern of markers and identifiable features that allowed replication of human activity with some guarantee of outcome.

MAPS IN MIND

There were also the images of space that were marked in the *minds* of a people — what today we call "cognitive" maps. Beyond static recreations of place, beyond the marking of a physical place, cognitive maps were at the very heart of aboriginal cultures. People who lived in place required a mental system that ordered information about an incredible amount of physical and ecological detail: where to hunt; where protection from invaders was best found; what plants were edible or medicinal, and where they could be reliably located; the location of trails, dens of dangerous animals, fords, lookouts, places of protection from weather, and fuel for heating. This purely spatial dimension of knowledge was made even more complex by the need to perceive how the element of time affected each phenomenon. Hunting varied with seasons and the longer cycles of a species' decline and rise. Plants are in varied abundance at different times of the year. Trails and fords are closed in certain types of weather.

Yet another dimension to this knowledge is that many aboriginal peoples were extremely mobile, migrating across huge physical and psychic distances. The ability to map territory into a sustaining familiarity was thus not just the work of sedentary folk. People in new surroundings had to evolve techniques of observation and learning that provided immediate sustenance from new environments. This ability to know a new place quickly and well, and to adapt to its circumstance, may be the most important unique attribute of the human animal.

Imagine a world where your people have lived for scores of generations. You know where every source of sustenance is, in what quantities, and in what season. You travel widely to make this annual cycle of harvest. Paths are etched on the ground. Places which best offer shelter in different seasons are worn hard. There is a rhythm to the seasonal round, predictable as much as circumstance allowed. And occasionally there would be exploration of new territories, journeys empowered by the honing of skills that brought confidence to go beyond the purely familiar.

The process of relating time and space in a defined territory created a potent coevolution. From what were at first purely the needs of survival, there grew a primal need to somehow understand why and how the world "worked." Myths, legends, religions, philosophy and science all evolved from skills learned in relating perceptions of time and space to the needs of region-based human populations to survive.

It is in the realm of cognitive knowledge that true bioregional mapping dwells. For the primary defining factor of a bioregional culture will be the understanding that individuals, and larger associations of humans, must evolve an acute understanding of the nuance and supporting capability of place. This understanding, or rediscovery, of what was the standard way of human life for thousands of years affirms the power of the bioregional vision — it is not a new invention, but a memory that has only been briefly tranquilized.

The key to building empowering cognitive maps of bioregions is based entirely upon experience in the landscapes and ecosystems of place. If we cocoon ourselves in hermetically-sealed homes and offices, travel in locked cars at speeds that blur sight, turn culture into "input," and trade growth and harvest of food for the unwrapping of packages, we also atrophy an understanding of the forces which support us. When land and ecosystems and weather become invisible abstractions, we tolerate the destruction of these essential webs of life much more easily. It is through this spiral of dissociation that the planet has been plundered.

SONGS, DREAMS, AND GENERATIONS ON THE LAND

It is perhaps fitting that surviving aboriginal peoples are in many ways in the forefront of contemporary bioregional mapping. Cognitive knowledge of place preserved in language, myth, legend, and experience is being translated into graphic map images. The Inuit, already mentioned as having a long cartographic tradition, continue to be the focus of some of the most innovative contemporary mapping. In the mid-1970s two extraordinary studies were undertaken to graphically describe the spatial distribution of Inuit land use. *The Inuit Land Use and Occupancy Project* and *Our Footprints Are Everywhere: Inuit Land Use and Occupancy in Labrador* describe how teams of researchers interviewed Inuit people so as to understand their concept and use of their Arctic territories. What emerged from these studies is a glimpse of traditional cultures perhaps never before achieved. Instead of Western interpretations of Arctic society, the studies present scores of maps which simply show patterns of land use — etchings which together mark the truth of a magical adaptation to place. In the 1990s, innovative mapping continues to originate in the Arctic. The Tungavik Federation of Nunavut has published the *Nunavut Atlas*, a comprehensive series of land use maps which played a critical role in the creation of Nunavut, Canada's newest territory.

Prominent in the earlier Inuit studies is the work of Hugh Brody, an English polymath who understood that the best way to augment the map images was to use quotes from the Inuit themselves. Brody was obviously moved by this experience, and has continued to work on behalf of aboriginal peoples. His *Maps and Dreams* is an excellent introduction to the challenges of achieving cross-cultural understanding using maps as a focus of contact. *The Songlines* by the late Bruce Chatwin is another book that chronicles this type of adventure, as a gifted narrator moves into the spiritual and spatial dream worlds of Australian aborigines.

In a small region of northwestern British Columbia, an equally impressive range of bioregional mapping is in progress. The Nisga'a people have located the boundaries of extended family territories and, with a team of trained local interviewers, have marked hundreds of place names in the Nisga'a language. More recently, the Nisga'a purchased state of the art Geographic Information System (GIS) computer software and are now digitizing satellite images of their territory to defend sovereignty, and aid in the stewardship of locally controlled forests, fisheries, and other resources.

The Gitksan and Wet'suwet'en, neighbors of the Nisga'a, have also recorded traditional knowledge of their territory by interviewing Elders. The geographic information collected was eventually used as a primary source to make an atlas representing a collective image of how Gitksan and Wet'suwet'en people inhabit and steward their territory. The maps, created with the assistance of one of Canada's most skilled cartographers, Mr. Louis Skoda, were put on public display in Hazelton, British Columbia, in November 1990. They were an immensely popular attraction: for once here was an atlas that didn't represent a government or corporate scheme to pillage the land. Instead, a beautifully crafted set of images described home: how people migrated to their present territories, the meaning of ancient place names, where berries grow, and where to catch salmon.

The atlas and place name research done by the Gitksan and Wet'suwet'en is being used as an underpinning for a legal challenge against imposed Canadian control over their territories. Although this court challenge is still being fought, the Gitksan and Wet'suwet'en atlas hints that its outcome is perhaps not critical. Sovereignty is not entirely a commodity that is returned by a court of the usurpers. Those who know the land, who live on the land, will ultimately be its stewards.

This evolution of goals, from simple challenges to the assertion of control regardless of sanction by centralized government, is a lesson for residents of all bioregions. The Nisga'a and Gitksan and Wet'suwet'en have always known more about their territories than government or business interests. With the artful mix of cognitive and "modern" mapping techniques, they are now able to use this knowledge in a manner which absolutely confounds the juggernaut of civilization. The efficient deployment of rootless capital simply cannot adapt to an environment where an informed and confident non-transient culture demands that local limits and potentials be respected.

AN EVOLVING ATLAS OF HOME

This is only the barest of introductions to the lessons that aboriginal mapping can have for reinhabitants. If you read some of the books that have been cited, you'll get a better idea of the power that maps have in rooted societies. The next step would be to investigate the aboriginal peoples who have lived, or who still do live in your bioregion, and to find out how they conceptualized the folds and flows of your territory. You may seek out information through books, or if you are fortunate, it may be an incentive to speak with people you otherwise may not likely meet — those who never left.

Imagine this. In the town hall of your community a large atlas that describes "home" in a great variety of ways is prominently displayed. It has several hundred pages that depict layers of biophysical and cultural knowledge: climate, soils, flora and fauna, historic places, wind patterns, how much food was harvested by place and year, plus a summary of a host of related community experience. It is a well-worn tome, referred to continuously by local citizens. In the margins are pencilled notes, adding new information to that which is already shown. Every year or so, your community updates the atlas, growing another layer to the collective understanding of the potentials and limits of place. On the evening that each new edition of the atlas is unveiled, Elders are invited to "speak" each map, adding stories to further animate the wisdom that the flat pages tell. There are songs, dances, and ribald stories, all relating to the occupation of a well-loved territory. It is entertainment and celebration on one level; on another, it is an absolutely critical validation of larger community potential and purpose. This is the role mapping plays in the bioregional vision.

3

Mapping
the Experience of Place

♦

Introduction

Doug Aberley

People often talk about how our communities and regions, or the world, can be changed. Unfortunately many folk don't get beyond *talking* about change — they are well-meaning, but defeated by cynicism or inertia. This part of our exploration of local mapping is about people and organizations who have overcome this *ennui*. Across this spinning, imperfect sphere, local people are making truly inspiring efforts to "walk the mapping talk."

For nearly twenty years people living in place have been developing mapping skills. Although there is no exact history of this process, it is possible to briefly highlight some of the more memorable images that have been used to define and defend the bioregional vision.

The first bioregional maps were created in 1973 by Raymond Dasmann and Miklos Udvardy as part of a United Nations study of global biotic provinces. *CoEvolution Quarterly* magazine later reprinted one of these images which enjoyed great popularity. In the mid-1970s the Planet Drum Foundation used maps to illustrate a reinhabitory vision for California. Peter Berg and Judy Goldhaft from Planet Drum have continued to use maps artfully to illustrate their periodical *Raise the Stakes*, a prime source of bioregional inspiration. Then, in 1977, *CoEvolution Quarterly* published a map of the mini-nationalities of Europe, an image which emphasized the bio*cultural* roots of bioregionalism. From the 1980s onward there have been a host of bioregion maps created — most notably for Hudsonia, the Sonoran bioregion, and the Ozarks. In Cascadia, David McCloskey has been especially instrumental in drawing a bioregion into being. David's images, along with similar maps drawn by Bob Benson and Cameron Suttles, have been used with great effect in helping people to perceive the shape and promise of bioregionalism. In 1985 the first systematic method of describing the external and internal characteristics of a bioregion was proposed using Northwest British Columbia as an example; revised over the years, it is included in the form of a primer as Chapter 5 of this volume.

During the five North American Bioregional Congresses that have been held biannually since 1984, the mapping workshop has become increasingly popular. At the 1992 Congress, upwards of twenty people participated in discussions that included a review of scores of map images. Most of the sheets that were on display were not made especially for bioregional purposes, but they were valuable nonetheless in conceptualizing territories defined by soil, water, and culture. This is the joy of looking for home; through the inspired work of cartographers and researchers with names such as Demarchi, Skoda, Krajina, Bailey, Küchler, Omernick and others, there begins to emerge a bioregional rhythm to the landscape (see Chapter 6 for complete references). Images made for a variety of unrelated purposes can be combined into a potent vision for a sustainable future.

The articles in this chapter all record peoples' actual experience with mapping projects, and separate into three general categories. First are stories of bioregional mapping in urban settings. With over 70 percent of North Americans living in urban settlements, there can be no doubt that our vision of a sustainable future must answer to how cities can be transformed. Next come tales of mapping in rural regions. Of special note are the contributions from the United Kingdom. Finally, two contributors explain the use of computer mapping software — known as Geographic Information Systems (GIS) — as it is being employed at the grassroots level. From Chicago, to the southwest of England, to the west slope of the Sierra — home-made images of place are emerging in great diversity.

Mapping is playing an important role in the continuing evolution of community and bioregional purpose. People who have grown through a long series of experiences are using maps to communicate the responsibilities of the reinhabitant's path. This is very much the process of becoming powerful in place: small steps taken, with the positive results used to take larger steps. From just thinking about the worth of maps, to conceptualizing how they might look, to actually taking pen to paper, we can use maps as a means to celebrate, to defend, and to empower legitimacy.

Welcome to the world of those who have migrated from the intent to do mapping, to the realm of actual mapping practice. Technical and area-specific language has been interpreted as best as possible. The care these folk have for their homes and planet requires no interpretation at all.

♦

Mapping the Wild Onion Bioregion

Beatrice Briggs

Committed to helping city dwellers discover their connections to the natural world without necessarily leaving the urban environment, Beatrice Briggs is a founder of the Wild Onion Alliance. Deceptively rural in name, this bioregional group originates from deep in the heart of the city of Chicago. A resident of Chicago since 1971, Beatrice describes here the breakthrough that the creation of a map for their region brought to their organizing efforts.

The Wild Onion Bioregion, more commonly known as greater metropolitan Chicago, lies on the glacial lake plain at the southwestern tip of Lake Michigan and in the watersheds of the Chicago, DesPlaines, Fox and Calumet Rivers. Once tallgrass prairie, oak savannah and wetlands, the land is now heavily urbanized. The name "Wild Onion" refers to *Allium cernuum*, or nodding wild onion. One of several native species of *Allium*, these plants are believed to be what the Potowatami referred to when they called this place "che-cau-gou," or "place of the strong smells."

The Wild Onion Alliance, our local bioregional organization, was born at a one-day conference, "Re-Inhabiting Chicago: A Bioregional Perspective," in February, 1989. We publish a newsletter, *Downwind*, place articles, poetry and artwork in other area publications, sponsor field trips, celebrate the solstices and equinoxes with rituals grounded in the realities of our home place, encourage the singing of songs and the telling of stories about the bioregion, provide speakers and information tables at eco-events, and support the work of other grassroots organizations in our area. We are part of the recently formed Turtle Island Network of bioregional resource centers and hosts of Chicago's 1993 Great Lakes Bioregional Congress.

For the first four years of our existence, we had an evolving description, but no adequate map, of our bioregion. The watersheds of the four rivers which we named as our "borders" flow through three states and a dozen counties. The maps we found tended to end abruptly at county or state lines. This frustrating situation convinced us of the power of maps to shape our thinking about the natural world. How can we be expected to relate to something like a watershed or a bioregion if we cannot even find it on a map?

In some ways, we benefitted from the lack of a map. Because we were not tied to any specific depiction of our bioregion, we had to "live with," and revise, our definition of the land of the wild onion. At first, in our ignorance, we designated the Little Calumet River as the southeastern border of the bioregion. This river lies conveniently within the boundaries of Illinois, but is an integral part of a much larger hydrological system, most of which is in Indiana. Eventually we woke up to this reality and knew that our map, when we got one, would have to include all of the Calumet River. We were also puzzled by how to treat the rivers, such as the Kankakee, Wabash and Vermillion, which lie outside of our micro-region, but which are clearly part of the same watershed as the Fox and the DesPlaines. Would not cutting off those rivers from each other be just as arbitrary and disrespectful of the natural features of the land as the despised state and county maps? Where and how does one draw the line?

In addition to these thorny intellectual questions, our efforts to acquire a map raised equally challenging technical and financial considerations. Our investigations all seemed to lead toward the U.S. Geological Survey (USGS) maps as being the best source for the information we wanted to show. Another local organization had spent $2,000 on USGS negatives, and an additional $5,000 on cartography to produce a first-rate map of area bicycle trails. Although we were offered the use of those negatives for a minimal fee, they did not include the whole area we wished to show. Furthermore, we lacked the funds needed to convert the negatives into a usable map. More frustration.

Finally, in mid-December, 1992, at the suggestion of one of our members, we contacted historian David Buisseret at the Newberry Library, a private research facility in Chicago which has excellent cartographic materials. Buisseret readily grasped our dilemma and introduced us to his assistant and chief cartographer, Tom Willcockson. Willcockson, in turn, agreed to produce a map for a $300 freelance fee during his Christmas vacation. Thus, by early 1993, we had an affordable map, drawn on computer to our specifications, which would meet our immediate educational needs and which would also serve as a base map for the overlays we eventually hope to commission. These proposed overlays include: a surface geology map, showing the moraines of our once heavily glaciated area; a map showing the forest cover, wetlands and primary Indian settlements before the arrival of the Europeans; and a series of maps tracing the history of population growth and development which, since 1832, has transformed a land rich in everything from microbes to large mammals into a vast parking lot.

And how did we solve the problem of how to map our bioregion, without either expanding its boundaries beyond what felt to be "right" or ignoring the very real connection between "our" rivers and the others which join them in the journey to the Gulf of Mexico? Our cartographer suggested showing the entire watershed of the Upper Illinois Valley, and then identifying the Wild Onion Bioregion within that context. Once we saw the map drawn in this way, we were dismayed that we had not seen this elegant, truthful solution before. All we needed was a good map to teach us some important lessons about the place we call home.

Where Are We? Who Are We? Mapping an Urban Bioregion

Whitney Smith

Still in the process of completing the map of their bioregion, activists in the Oak Ridges Bioregion have used existing resources and creative incentives to propel their project further along the path to completion. Whitney Smith from Toronto — a social entrepreneur developing projects that promote bioregional and community economic development strategies, and artistic Director of the Society for the Preservation of Wild Culture — describes their progress so far.

After a few years of struggling with the question of how to promote bioregionalism in my local megalopolis, I realized that it was more a matter of putting together what already existed than creating something new. In some ways, bioregionalism is like puzzle-making: piecing together the many fragments of a region into an aesthetic, enduring picture that we can point to and say, "We live here and we love it!" For each community though, these pieces will be different and will go together differently: ecological restoration may be more relevant or urgent in a given community than social justice, economics, public health, daycare, or literacy. Ecological restoration may not matter at all. Whatever the waiting line of needs, there is one thing that is fundamental: each place requires pivot points, *coordinates*, that define it in the minds of its citizens — images, myths, repertoires of songs or stories — living culture, not theory, that anchors commonality.

As activists navigating through weird waters, we are always seeking these coordinates. They lead us somewhere. They lead to create, and unearth, solidarity: through rallies and demonstrations, conferences and picnics, pamphlets and videos, lectures and workshops, circles and alliances. As bioregionalists, as activists of place and small "e" earth, our primary coordinates must be ones that answer the questions of "Where?" and "Who?" The other questions about issues and method, the "what is broken" and "how we can fix it," are part of every region's concerns, but it is these images and stories — symbols and belonging — that formed our sense of place.

Producing these things is very easy and very hard. Stories and songs that evoke the genuine spirit of a place can happen spontaneously, in a minute. As well, they cannot be willed. You can put the word out — "Indigenous Songs and Stories Wanted! Old and new!" — and wait, but the muses will not be bribed with juicy grants. Images, however — especially the most popular kind, maps — *can* be submitted to a critical path, and to produce an image of our megaloporegion, the Oak Ridges Bioregion which measures 130 kilometres by 25 kilometres, and contains 30 watersheds and 4.5 million people, we chose to concentrate on producing a map that would do something (*anything!*) to focus the urban sprawling mind.

Our work on this map, which is still in progress, came by way of a conference organized in the spring of 1992, called "Our Own Back Yard: Toronto Bioregion Week" (see *Raise The Stakes* #20, 1992). The purpose of the conference was to coordinate ecological renewal efforts in the region. At the conference we told our "stories" and sang our "songs" — lectures, panels, workshops and dances, inexpensive and gourmet indigenous feasts, and organic farm tours — all in an effort to seed the bioregional idea.

The stories worked, but what we didn't have was a good image, a good map, a picture that said "home." What we did have was a map of the Greater Toronto Bioregion produced by an enlightened federal commission on the future of the Toronto waterfront (now called the Regeneration Trust) that showed the boundaries of the bioregion formed by an escarpment, a long moraine, and a (Great) lake. This was a basic watershed map that, following the conference, was filled in with several details and published in a local magazine. This map included greenlands, aboriginal sites, wildlife features, and more. Its publication had a significant effect on public awareness. People began to understand that they didn't just live in a city. They realized that a bioregion was a place where many things were considered.

In an effort to get a comprehensive bioregional map that showed various perspectives (landform and land use, climate, natural heritage, anthropology and historical demography, cultural and political regions, and so on) we suggested a map project for the bioregion to the Regeneration Trust. This map would be part of a proposed integrated information project that is now called "BRAIN." This Bioregional Research And Information Network would access different banks of information on computer for government, business, environmental and community sectors in the bioregion. The map would be an integrated component of this system, a graphic representation of local data that would be interactive with BRAIN data.

In the best of all possible economies, this coordinated map could be a powerful and practical tool for managing an ecosystem effectively — perhaps even at the citizen level. With maps that used GIS (Geographic Information System), there is no end to how evolved our knowledge of our communities could be. And no end to expense either — GIS projects easily jump into the millions. Therefore our solution to preparing a map now, rather than writing lots of proposals about it, was to hold a competition, open to university departments (geography, landscape architecture, urban and regional planning, environmental studies, agriculture, and research management), for the best reasonably comprehensive map of our newly-named area, the Oak Ridges Bioregion — all for considerably less than a million bucks. From our conversations with various levels of government, we feel there is a good chance that they will pay for the printing and distribution of such a map. If not, to *market to market*...

Whatever the method or timetable, a graphic image of our bioregion will get made and get known. If not by us, by someone else who seeks another tool for action; something that can make the links, be beautiful,

and reconnect us to nature and place, intellectually and emotionally —
an icon to inspired bioregional ideals. Or, just a new map because maps
are fun. Whatever the reasons, the doing of it will bring a lot of us closer
to home.

◆

Evolving Visions of Place

Doug Sherriff and Eleanor Wright

*Ever-encroaching clearcut logging has prompted one community in British
Columbia's interior to develop mapping techniques that aim to preserve species
diversity as much as possible within the business-as-usual regime. Practiced
outdoorsman, Doug Sherriff, and Eleanor Wright, a co-editor of the book* Home:
A Bioregional Reader!, *give an overview of their experience to date.*

Our small rural community is situated in a bioregion in the southern interior of British Columbia with Lillooet as the local town.
The region is characterized by a very dry climate. This, combined with
steep mountain topography and frequent forest fires, has resulted in an
extremely diverse forest structure composed of islands of old forest
surrounded by a mosaic of younger stands. Grasslands and deciduous
groves are infrequently interspersed within the forest. Though the region is very sparsely populated and ownership of the vast majority of
the land is vested in the state, that which is privately owned is the most
biologically productive and sensitive. The economy of the region is
almost exclusively fueled by natural resource extraction, the best wood
produced by the forests being the prime contributor. Minerals, agricultural products, recreation, and service industries make minor individual
contributions, though when combined, they come close to equalling the
timber interests. Undocumented, but clearly significant, is the self-suffi-
cient informal economy of the region, enabled by good growing conditions, a history of fluctuating mainstream prosperity, and an ongoing
influx of refugees from urban industrial centers.

That's who we all were originally. Now we call this place home. For many years our main focus has been on creating and nurturing the essentials of our domestic scenes, including our evolving community. It has come naturally to us to learn about the wild plant and animal communities that surround us as we walk, ride, camp, gather firewood, harvest berries and herbs, fish, hunt and find spiritual renewal in the wild places around us.

In the early '80s we became conscious of ourselves as living within a "bioregion." We are reinhabitants of an area traditionally used by the Stl'atl'imx Nation for hunting and gathering, and subsequently severely damaged by the miners, hunters, loggers, agriculturalists and hydro producers. Self-government has been one of our themes for many years and is realized in the form of a community council which meets monthly. Defense of our homeland has been handled by our ecological society, inspired greatly by the idea "think globally, act locally." Over the years we've been amassing details in our own "bioregional study," and have dabbled some in mapping. But three years ago something happened which brought into focus the need for some urgent mapping of the biotic communities of this watershed.

At that time, the British Columbia Ministry of Forests proposed to access and exploit over half of our 110,000 hectare watershed within a five year period, with more to follow. As a community council representing the "Local Resident Public" we approached the Forest Service and the sawmill operators and demanded a long-term management plan with public involvement and multiple resource-user-participation. Our bottom line was to guarantee ecosystem integrity and the maintenance of biotic diversity within our watershed, while allowing sustainable resource extraction to proceed using the new ecological forest practices.

One of the basic tenets of these new practices is to plan ecologically on a landscape or creekshed scale; of course, this requires knowledge about creeksheds and what's in them. A very few simple questions at district and regional forestry offices, as well as at the sawmill, quickly convinced us that the people who should know these things did not. We determined therefore to learn them ourselves, so that we could know what to protect during the course of the Local Resource Use Plan they offered us.

We have mapped within our watershed the distribution and abundance of those factors highly important to ecosystem function, such as plant community types, winter ranges and other habitat features, and the location of rare species. Our method is not intended to be definitive, but rather to narrow down with available information just where to go looking within a large area for certain high value or rare ecosystem types.

Because this mapping system requires ground verification, we appreciate the fact that it allows us to predict the nature of the vegetation in isolated parts of our watershed, saving a lot of wasted effort in our search for really rare or critical areas before actually going there. We have used air photos, topographic maps, biogeoclimatic maps, ecosystem classification data, and forest cover maps. More detailed information about our methods is available from the Yalakom Watershed Study, Box 1105, Lillooet, BC, V0K 1V0.

A critical starting point is to properly gauge the scale of mapping you require for the job you wish to do. We chose to map our watershed with a fineness of grain sufficient to compare the attributes of the creeksheds of five to 10,000 hectares in size within it. This scale allows us to compare our watershed with any other watershed of similar size for which similar data is available. Industry and forest services have little desire to see data of this scale, and techniques such as these implemented. Available information is usually very coarse-grained, suitable for regional- or provincial-scale questions, or, at the other extreme, useful only at the individual timber stand level.

The critical problems of today are ecosystem-scale problems. The flow of life within landscapes is seldom examined before it is disturbed, and this is reflected by the information available for any given place. The major difficulty we have had to overcome has been adjusting these scale differences and integrating inventory systems that have been designed in isolation from one another. This has required considerable study of such systems, and the theory of ecosystem function.

The data we have gathered in map form provides a very useful tool for planning future changes to the landscape. It also helps citizens groups such as ours to inject some concepts from conservation biology into local resource decisions. By mapping important ecosystem attributes as they exist today in our place, and continuing to map the changes in them as they occur, we build the framework for effective and accurate description of the biological impoverishment that is inevitable if our conservation efforts of today are inadequate.

Although funding has been delayed, there is a plan afoot to do a bioregional study of the Lillooet area. We hope that the mapping work we have done in our watershed will serve as a basis for similar work in the rest of the bioregion.

A simplified version of our methodology has been used by a friend in the Williams Lake Forest Region to map 190,000 hectares. She isolated the mature and developed Douglas fir stands in this large area, quantified their present distribution and abundance, and very effectively illustrated their rapid elimination through past and present logging practices and faulty land-use planning strategies. She and her friends were successful in having the unique area brought under consideration as an ecosystem reserve.

One final thought: no amount of mapping can be useful unless we talk with the spirits of the place before, during, and after the exercise in abstraction which a mapping project necessarily is.

Putting Dartia on the Map

Kirkpatrick Sale

The growing excitement that people feel as a bioregion emerges from ongoing mapping work is a commonly related phenomenon. Kirkpatrick Sale, a founding member of the Hudson Bioregional Council and the North American (now Turtle Island) Bioregional Congress, and author of Dwellers in the Land: The Bioregional Vision, *shares a recent experience that seems to have inspired a truly international enthusiasm for such work.*

In the spring of 1992 I was asked to give a course on bioregionalism for the new Schumacher College, an innovative and experimental school that had been established in southwest England to examine and teach the ideas that had been propounded so ably by the author of *Small Is Beautiful* in the 1970s. I had naturally accepted — it meant being part of a line of such visiting scholars as James Lovelock, Hazel Henderson, Jonathan Porritt, and Arne Naess — but I hadn't the least idea about how I'd actually go about teaching the complex ideas of bioregionalism to the several dozen students normally attracted there, and in just two weeks at that.

I finally decided that we'd divide it into two parts: in the mornings, for three hours or so, I would give lectures on the theoretical aspects of bioregionalism, based largely on my own *Dwellers in the Land*, and in the afternoons I would have the students compile the statistics, learn the history and lore, and tramp the countryside to assemble a map of the very bioregion in which the college was located. That way, I figured, they could be doing something practical, something useful, in fact, for the people of the college and surrounding area, and something that would teach them how to go back to their own homes and transpose the ideas and techniques of bioregionalism there.

By "map," I had something quite special in mind: an exercise that I had often wanted to see carried out in the Hudson Valley, my own bioregion. I envisaged not just the outline, the "borders" of the region, although even that begins to help people understand the actual patterning of nature, but more: an inventory of the species of the area (floral, and faunal, including human), and where they were located. Also to be included was an inventory of the ways that resources had been historically used by the people of the region and were being used by people today, and if possible, some sort of export-import analysis to indicate how far from the conditions of self-sufficiency they had come.

It was a tall order, of course, but everyone who signed up for the course knew that such a project was being planned and would be asked to participate as best they could. And with nothing more than that, I set off for England.

Schumacher College is located in Dartington, near the little town of Totnes, on the banks of the River Dart which runs from the hills of Dartmoor in western Devon down to, obviously, Dartmouth on the shore of the English Channel. As soon as I got there, I asked for geological survey maps of the area, at several scales, and right away it became apparent that the easiest, and probably most accurate, way to establish the bioregion was the watershed of the Dart, an area about 40 miles long and from 10 to 20 miles wide. I explained to the class — a dozen paying students, from all parts of England, Hungary, Czechoslovakia, and India, plus a floating number of college staff members — that our task was to fill in the map of the Dart watershed, or "Dartia" as we named it, with as much information as we could get.

And so every afternoon was devoted to amassing as much as we could learn about Dartia from libraries, government offices, local experts, and the like: native flora and fauna, climate, soil types, hydrology, geology, and resources, on the one hand — that is, what was naturally *there* — and land use, agriculture, settlements, building types, manufacturing, fishing, and resource use, on the other — that is, how humans dealt with what was there. We also went on as many field trips as our meager budgets allowed: to Dartmoor, to the shore, and on a boat ride from Totnes to Dartmouth. We also invited in several local experts, including the public information officer from the Dartmoor National Park, the head of planning of the local district council, the head of the local Totnes museum, and a local historian and former Totnes mayor.

Not everyone was equally enthusiastic about the task, especially when it turned out that the sources of information were so few and, often, so inadequate, and real ingenuity had to be exercised to fill in the necessary gaps. But some took to it with real avidity: the Czech woman whose passion was flowers and who devised an elaborate map and chart of the native flora, divided into upland and lowland species; the Scot who went everywhere to determine rainfall and water flows, as well as present energy use and future alternative-energy possibilities; the Indian woman who examined building materials in the region, both historically and at present, with a map of where they were located, labeled "D'Art of Buildings;" and the retired English architect who did a beautiful topographical map and soil and land-use analysis, up to all hours of the night.

As the material began to flow in, two things became clear. First, we would have to assemble a *series* of maps, each one devoted to the particular subject at hand, rather than try to put all the information on a single sheet, and the end product would be a booklet. Fortunately, we also had a keen computer programmer

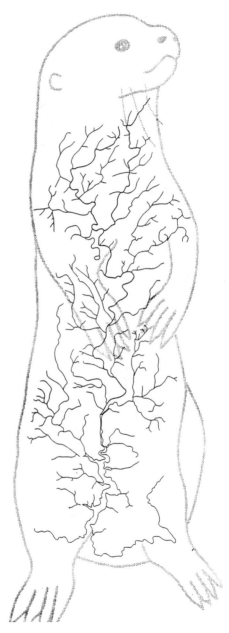

Dartia The Otter

who had brought his own machine and was able to transform the raw data into a series of identically-shaped maps, looking as if they were printed, with the information presented in an artful visual fashion. Second, we would somehow have to convey what we had learned about how the bioregion originally functioned before the industrial transformations of the 19th and 20th centuries, and how it might therefore work towards self-sufficiency in the future with local resources and energy flows. Fortunately for *this*, we had several people avid to suggest what a future bioregion would look like in terms of clothing, shelter, water use, food, employment and the like, and they wrote up paragraphs that were superimposed on a large-scale version of the basic map.

Then one of the women, at first hesitant but increasingly eager as she got into the project, discovered that the outline of Dartia, with just a little imagination and just a few lines, could be made into the exact image of a standing otter — a beloved animal special to the area and so, of course, our perfect "totem." We assembled all this on the last night of the class, photocopied a whole bunch of them, and then on the final day I went with one of the students to present the booklet — with a handsome cover, a sketch of "Dartia the Otter," a short explanation of bioregionalism, four charts, and sixteen maps — to the local townspeople, an idea that had only occurred to us at the end. We enlisted the local newspaper and its photographer and then delivered copies to the Totnes library, the Totnes museum, the head of the district council, and to one of the local green/permaculture centers. Bemused they all were, of course, but they all saw that we had a vision for the valley they loved, and had done some serious homework about how to think about making it a reality.

I can't say if the people of Dartia have subsequently taken to the idea of their valley as a bioregion or of the ways it might learn to live healthily and prosperously on its own resources. I do know that the article in the local newspaper was full and fair, and indicated that the recipients of the booklet were enthusiastic. I also know that the people at the college itself generally seemed keen on the idea of bioregionalism, now that they had learned what it looked like in some concrete form. They also understood themselves for the first time as being connected to Totnes and its region, as citizens of a bioregion.

And the dozen students I know went away with a new sense of how they fit into the world and how they might develop the potentials of the places they call home — and that is all bioregionalism could hope to do, really. Just last week in the mail I got a letter from one of the students, back home in India. "I noticed a lot of significant changes in me," he wrote, "because of the fascinating idea of the concept of bioregionalism

... and the necessity of its replicability." He added that he had written several articles on bioregionalism in Hindi for local publications, and had delivered a paper on his own area as a bioregion for an international conference in Delhi. He also invited me to his valley to see how they were beginning to put bioregionalism into practice there; but I can see that he doesn't need me anymore. After all, he has Dartia.

Copies of Dartia: The Dart Valley Bioregion *may be purchased for US$10.00 or £5 from Schumacher College, Dartington, Totnes, Devon TQ9 6EA, U.K.*

Mapping Your Roots: Parish Mapping

Angela King

Making every local person an expert has been one of the guiding principles of an English group that has successfully inspired hundreds of communities to map their familiar territories in truly unique ways. Angela King, a habitat and species conservationist, is a founding director and coordinator, with Sue Clifford, of Common Ground, the organization that has brought new life to the term "parish" in the work that they promote.

Common Ground's Parish Maps Project starts with the simple question, "What do you value in your place?" This puts everyone in the role of expert. It was launched in 1985 with the purpose of encouraging people to share information about their localities and to record aspects they cared about. At a time of such rapid change, both in town and country, it is important that the feelings of local people about the places where they live are taken into consideration. Too often, valued features and places are lost by default.

In the five years since the project began, around a thousand maps have been made by parish councils, schools, women's groups, and individuals. The form they have taken has varied, and has included the use of textiles, ceramics, photographs, a newspaper, paint and song. The stipulation that the maps can be made by anyone and in whatever form has

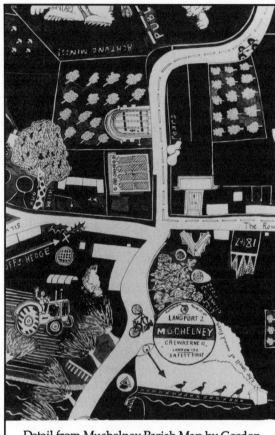

Detail from Muchelney Parish Map by Gordon
Young, 1989 – part of Common Ground's
Parish Maps Project.

been an important reason for the tremendous response. The mappers haven't felt constrained by traditional mapping techniques or by the impersonal formality of the Ordnance Survey (which makes the U.K. topographic maps). Idiosyncrasy and variety have been encouraged. Common Ground sees the process of map-making as the start of a greater involvement with one's place; once we become more aware of our surroundings, it becomes easier to conserve them.

It seems only natural that we should value most what we are in contact with every day — local and familiar places, commonplace birds and buildings — yet the reverse is often true. We appear to put higher value on rare animals and plants, spectacular buildings, and far-flung places. Of course, all are important because they fulfil different needs. But the everyday places desperately need our attention because they are changing so fast and not always for the better, because everywhere is beginning to look the same, and because much benefit can be gained from a personal involvement with our localities.

Whether we live in a town or in the country, there are always things around us which are important in our everyday life. Perhaps there are buildings — a mill or a warehouse, a bridge or disused railway station

— which reflect the lives of the people who lived in the area before us. Perhaps we enjoy a walk along lanes lined with primrose in spring, through water meadows, or wild fells grazed by sheep. A favorite walk may take you beside a canal, or along banks of a stream, or beside old stone walls. These are details which give our area their own distinctive character.

We have no word in English to express *Heimat* in German, or *bro* or *cynefin* in Welsh, meaning familiar territory. But Common Ground is offering the word "parish" as a substitute. A parish, often based on ancient ecclesiastical delineations, is the smallest political and administrative unit recognized by central government in the United Kingdom. But Common Ground is using the word in a looser sense to mean the locality to which people feel a sense of belonging and which belongs to them. People can draw their own lines, or use old ecclesiastical or newer civil parish or community council boundaries.

Through making maps we can identify what our place has to offer and what aspects of it need more attention. For example, whether we have access to a good local network of footpaths; whether there is an abundance of wildlife and habitats — unfertilized meadows, heathland, wetland, deciduous woodland and abandoned corners in the city. Are the vernacular buildings in the area in good repair? Is the history of the landscape recognized and protected? Could land — a meadow, orchard, pocket park or allotment — be owned by the parish for community use? What makes your place different from the next? How can you reinforce local distinctiveness and detail? Do you know where the parish boundary goes? If it follows banks and hedges, these features could be very old and have historical and wildlife value that has accumulated over many centuries.

When these maps are publicly displayed they may stimulate others to look again at their surroundings, and to discuss and discover new ways of ensuring that ordinary but well-loved features are looked after.

As we hoped, many groups have used their maps as the starting point for showing that they are actively caring for their place. For example, in Chideock, Dorset, the map has inspired the compilation of photographic records of the village's streets, and fauna and flora footpath guides. In addition, the Chideock Society has been formed to fight local issues. A few miles further west, mappers in Uplyme printed their map and, with the proceeds from sales, have sown a wildflower meadow and commissioned the creation of a new stone village sign. In the process of making their map, Lockwood in Cleveland opened all their footpaths, and created a boundary walk. Sylvia Kelly in Bristol is using her map of

Detail of the Parish Map of Red Lynch, Wiltshire, 1987.
This unique map is made of tapestry.
Photo: Julian Germain, Common Ground.

Golden Hill to fight a plan by a supermarket to build on a valued area of open space which is also an oasis for wildlife.

Trees, hedgerows and ponds have been saved from destruction, old barns have been renovated, orchards taken into community use, and old festivals revived — all because people have rediscovered their richness while making a parish map. Many maps have also been turned successfully into posters or postcards, reaching more people and generating income which can be put directly toward conservation purposes.

Common Ground is currently promoting the idea of Parish Walks as a means of recognizing and discussing the features which make places different and distinct from each other. We have been delighted by the ingenuity and spirit of those who have made and orchestrated Parish Maps. There are so many more we should have wished to pay tribute to.

Let's hope that the process of making a Parish Map will be the beginning of a concerted fight to prevent the march of conformity and homogeneity across Britain. We have so much to celebrate — and so much to lose.

Common Ground can be reached at 41 Sheldon Street, London, U.K. WC2H 9HJ. Send £2.50 by International Money Order for a copy of Parish Maps, *a 19-page booklet describing how to make your own local map.*

Watersheds as Unclaimed Territories

Freeman House

Ecosystem restoration requires, first, that you are sufficiently familiar with your place to know what there is to work with. Pioneering the attempt to gather and map such baseline data has been the Mattole Restoration Council in northern California, Shasta Bioregion. Freeman House, a co-founder of the Council, describes what has become a model for such efforts.

By 1985, the Mattole Watershed Salmon Support Group had been implementing its backyard hatchery program for some years; capturing parent stock from the native king salmon in winter, incubating the eggs in spectacularly low-tech systems, and then releasing the fingerlings back into the wild. Even though the program resulted in an eight- to ten-fold increase in egg-to-fry survival, everyone involved knew that at best this was a stopgap measure to keep the native strain alive while the aquatic ecosystems recovered.

The Mattole Restoration Council (MRC) in northern California was created to establish a forum for the kind of watershed-wide decisions that would need to be made as habitat rehabilitation programs were designed. Environmental restorationists soon found themselves embroiled in land-use controversies. Hands-on experience in the creeks and on the slopes had made the workers supersensitive to some of the practices that had resulted in the damages they were repairing. Why go on if the same mistakes were being made on the next parcel upstream?

Historically, cut-and-run forestry practices had been the root cause of a large percentage of the trashed channels, riparian zones bereft of vegetation, and cemented gravels that we were observing. On rare ventures into the original stands of vegetation — old growth — anyone could see that this kind of damage was rare in the absence of human development. The notion began to grow that it might be a good idea to treat these isolated stands of old growth as islands of stability, and to work out from there toward the rehabilitation of habitat. Local environmentalists were creating constituencies for the protection of particular stands of ancient forest, but the effort tended to be hit-and-miss, and based on the presence of glamorous megaflora like redwoods, or on the sentiments of an entrenched community nearby.

Whether you are designing a rehabilitation plan or zoning for the enhancement of biodiversity, the obvious first step is to find out what's there now. This was to be our first exposure to the disturbing fact that, on private property (and often on public property, too), the biological baseline data simply wasn't there. When we began to inquire into the actual extent of the logging in the valley and the amount of old growth remaining, we quickly found that nobody knew. The large industrial landowners were foggy on the concept; the smaller landowners hadn't the time or money to monitor systematically, and the state acted as if no one had ever asked the question before. If we really needed know, and we did, we would have to do the mapping ourselves. Luckily, the L. J. and Mary C. Skaggs Foundation agreed with us.

As an inhabitory group dedicated to the principle that the design and implementation of environmental restoration projects is best done by local residents, we were delighted at the prospect of doing some systematic mapping of the larger home, the riverine watershed. We had already performed a watershed-wide inventory of salmonid habitat, many of us had been trained by Redwood National Park geologists in geomorphic mapping techniques, and all of us had years of experience poring over topographic maps of our local terrain. The project presented itself as an opportunity to deepen, systematize, and share our collective local knowledge and skills. We became determined to make two maps: one of the watershed in 1947, before any large-scale industrial harvest had occurred; and one for the present, to show how much of the original ecosystem was left intact.

We divided the 300-square mile watershed into twelve groups of tributaries, each less than 50,000 acres. In most areas, we were able to locate one or two local inhabitants who were familiar with the landscape surrounding their homes. We acquired for them aerial photos of the watershed shot by WAC Corporation of Eugene, Oregon. WAC flies western Oregon and northwestern California semi-annually and makes the photos available either for standard nine by nine inch stereo-optic viewing, or through custom enlargements for any area at any scale.

To map the original forest, we used Timber Stand and Vegetation Element Maps developed in the 1950s by the U.S. Forest Service, the state Department of Forestry, and the University of California. These maps fit our situation conveniently: they were based on 1947 aerial photos, our preferred comparison date. We also used the Timber Stand Map's criteria for old growth timber: area with trees over a hundred years old, more than a hundred feet tall, and with a crown cover density of at least five to forty percent. Later, as the research led by Jerry Franklin into the nature of old growth ecosystems became more widely known, we found that these definitions were less than adequate. This discrepancy led us to map areas on the present day map as old growth which didn't have all the characteristics of late seral stage succession. Other groups taking on similar projects in Douglas fir country can avoid this problem by consulting Franklin et. al., "Modifying Douglas fir management regimes for nontimber objectives."

In the period between 1960 and 1972, the county in which most of the Mattole is located had kept timber harvest inventory maps in order to administer an onerous and anti-ecological tax on standing timber. By copying and distributing these maps, we provided local surveyors with a starting point for locating stands of old growth in their area. Surveyors compared these maps with their 1984 aerial photos, consulted the MRC's files of post-1984 Timber Harvest Plans in the watershed, and filled in the gaps with ground-truthing expeditions in the field. This phase of the project was filled with a sense of exploration and discovery, of recognition and completion, as the map filled in like a particularly challenging jigsaw puzzle laid out on a very large table.

There followed a long and tedious period of preparing the product for print. A small cadre of artists, enthusiasts, and roadrunners struggled with standardizing various notetaking styles, discrepancies in scale, and problems of parallax as the pieces of the puzzle were enlarged or reduced xerographically. Computerized Geographic Information System software was still in its infancy at this time. Early in 1989, we were ready for the printer and out of money. Local tributary stewardship groups dug into their meager budgets, and some surveyors kicked back their stipends to allow us to print a poster of the map, in two colors, and mail it to every resident and landowner in the watershed, as well as to all the regulatory agencies which had anything to do with logging in the Mattole.

It is difficult to attribute cause-and-effect relationships between the map and what has occurred since, but there can be no doubt that it was a powerful tool. A durable watershed-based community has emerged through the empowering process of developing the information it needs to understand its situation. Some two-thirds of the old growth areas identified in the map have been afforded some measure of protection, and the disposition of the remaining one-third continues to be debated. In situations where there was public controversy, we often found ourselves cast in the role of expert, because we could provide a better large picture than the industrial landowners or the regulatory agencies.

The Mattole Restoration Council has gone on to develop maps of active sources of sedimentation in the Mattole, and is at work now monitoring and mapping hydrological processes in its estuary. These additions to the local literature allow rehabilitation projects to be practiced in their appropriate context, and provide local landowners with some of the information they need to plan their moves wisely. Systematic survey and notation has become a habit of mind for many local residents. Write-in-the-Rain notebooks and cameras have become as important a part of some canoe trips and creek hikes as sandwiches and canteens.

These days the air is full of news of the marvelous capabilities of GIS, a technological development that holds the threat of the capture of landscape information (and misinformation) by those who can afford the expensive machinery that collates and stores it. These wonderfully layered coloured pictures on softly lit screens can lull us into the illusion that we know more than we used to know about the ecological systems on which we depend. In California, as this is being written, the state's GIS program is still evolving in the direction of increased technological complexity, limited access for inhabitory non-professionals, and centralization of data distribution. In order for these ecological data banks to become a reflection of the fluid truths of living places, information is going to have to flow both ways. The struggle to counter the tendencies of this machinery to become a tool for the entrenchment of central control will necessarily be carried forward by communities immersed in the fabric of surrounding life — neighbors in boots and bluejeans often using pencils to produce the maps that allow for a future based on real knowledge.

The map described here can be purchased for US$2.50 U.S. postpaid from the Mattole Restoration Council , P.O. Box 160, Petrolia, CA 95558, U.S.A.

♦

Community-based Computer Mapping: The Yuba Experience

Kai Snyder

Because the future sustainability of our regions revolves around the politics of land use decisions made today, some situations call for us to be equipped with the kind of information available from highly sophisticated computer technology. Braving this new world, Kai Snyder, from the Yuba Watershed Institute in California, explains how new tools can be brought to the service of old struggles.

The Yuba river system drains part of the western slope of California's northern Sierra Nevada mountains. The climate is a compelling contrast of astringently hot, dry summers, and mild wet winters. Most of the people in the Yuba watershed live in the middle elevations among Ponderosa pine, Blue oak, Black oak, Douglas fir, and Madrone. Manzanita thrives, carpeting the clearcuts, old fire spots, and southern slopes.

Twenty years ago this area was reinhabited by a flurry of people escaping the city who formed a community living in hand-built cabins without electricity or telephones, and many without water. Even today few are on the power grid, but many have solar electricity which powers lights and computers. We like to joke that we've gone straight from the 19th to the 21st century.

Over the years, we've become very active in local and regional politics, fighting off proposed mining and development, appealing Forest Service timber sales, and learning the natural history of the area. Ironically, some local groups have begun to make use of complex, sophisticated computer mapping and analysis software, known as Geographic Information Systems (GIS), for addressing conservation and planning issues.

The Sierra Biodiversity Institute (SBI), a local non-profit organization focusing on the preservation of ancient forest in the Sierra Nevada, has been a leader in GIS conservation work. While attempting to locate remaining ancient forest before it was put up for sale, people at the institute discovered that the U.S. Forest Service hadn't compiled a comprehensive assessment of remaining older forests. The solution to this task was presented when, by chance, one of the members was interviewing a leading GIS manufacturer for a magazine article. After explaining the SBI's trouble in locating ancient forest, the computer company (ESRI) introduced them to Geographic Information Systems. Using the GIS and satellite imagery, they were able to select out the currently standing older forest. By the fall of 1991, they had not only identified all of the remaining ancient forest in each of the sierran National Forests, but they had also completed a proposal for a reserve system. Their maps are now being used in an effort to pass a national "western ancient forest protection bill."

Meanwhile, other people in the community had become interested in the Bureau of Land Management (BLM) parcels that are interspersed with our private lands. The possibility of clearcuts next door inspired negotiation with the BLM, and in the fall of 1990 a bioregional community group, the Yuba Watershed Institute, and a crafters' organization, the Timber Framers Guild, formed a cooperative management agreement with the BLM. The intent of the agreement is to foster the recovery of ancient forests, encourage research into and education about forest ecology, and to provide a small, sustainable harvest of quality timber. The 1200 acres of BLM land was named the 'Inimim Forest, after the Nisenan Indians' word for Ponderosa pine.

Using GIS, the Sierra Biodiversity Institute has assisted the Yuba Watershed Institute (YWI) in the creation of large-scale customized maps of the jointly managed BLM lands. Combining data from already existing, but previously uncompiled, maps, the YWI devised new maps showing the cooperative management area, parcel ownership and boundaries, soil types, and elevation contours. Also, a set of eight and one half by eleven inch paper maps for recording field data was created.

The SBI's Geographic Information System has also been helpful in the local planning process. Steve Beckwitt, a founder of the Sierra Biodiversity Institute, has created a series of maps for the purpose of county planning which illustrates and identifies such things as: the total number of undeveloped parcels and their distribution; population density based on the 1990 census; farmland based on the state's farmland classification; and habitat fragmentation. Beckwitt believes that GIS would be the most useful tool in a bioregional context for allocation of land use, and integrating sound ecological and economic planning.

GIS has many potential bioregional applications. Most obviously, it can be used to identify watershed boundaries. Arc/Info, the brand of GIS software produced by ESRI that the SBI uses, actually comes with a watershed boundary identification tool. GIS is also useful for demonstrating cause and effect chains within a watershed. For example, if it was apparent that bad logging practices have caused economic failure in rural areas, one might combine census data showing average family income with forest quality information over the past ten years to see if lower forest quality has been accompanied by lower average income. Another use of GIS would be to create a cohesive, ecologically sound watershed management plan. With GIS it becomes possible to integrate information from different people and disciplines at a broad scale, illuminating the larger picture and clarifying contradictory concerns. These types of analysis could be done in a bioregion-specific or watershed-specific context for meaningful bioregional planning.

While GIS has been very helpful for certain specific purposes here in the Yuba watershed, it is by no means an answer to all conservation or planning problems. GIS is a problem-solving tool and consequently, it is not helpful unless you have a job that requires it. As Gerry Mander notes, using technology is a potentially harmful personal choice that we can and should make conciously. GIS is certainly not something everyone needs to be familiar with. Whether GIS, or computers for that matter, could be considered "appropriate technology" is unlikely in a large time-frame. Nonetheless, GIS is playing a powerful role in our currently technocratic society, and hopefully it can be used as a tool that will allow us to acquire a deeper understanding of true bioregional planning.

For more information, contact The Yuba Watershed Institute, 17790 Tyler Foote Road, Nevada City, CA 95959, U.S.A.

◆

GIS in Friends of the Earth, U.K.: 1990s Technology Meets 1990s Needs

Jonathan Doig

Environmentalists in Europe and elsewhere are producing powerful and eloquent maps with the help of state of the art technology. Jonathan Doig specializes in Geographic Information Systems (GIS) because of their potential as a tool for environmental protection and management, and was GIS Manager at Friends of the Earth in London during 1991 and 1992. He brings us up to date on the shape of maps to come.

The foremost challenge of the 1990s is to transform society to meet the ecological imperatives of survival on a small planet. GIS—Geographic Information Systems — is a key tool for the job, and Friends of the Earth in the U.K. are making the most of the opportunity offered by this technology.

Global biodiversity is disappearing before we have even identified the majority of species. Here in the already biologically impoverished British Isles, our subsoil is contaminated with toxic waste; our rivers contain levels of dangerous chemicals which breach European law; under current policy our motor cars and power stations will continue to pollute the air both locally and globally well into the 21st century; and we maintain our stranglehold on Third World debt which is burdening developing countries and adding to the pressure for the future exploitation of their fragile environments. Strangely, however, none of this rated a mention in the recent U.K. election, which was contested on issues of taxation, education, health and electoral reform, with barely a whisper about the environment. Time is running out.

A litany of environmental disasters — Chernobyl, Bhopal, Exxon Valdez, Amazonian burning—and global crises such as ozone depletion and the greenhouse effect finally brought the planetary ecological situation to the attention of people throughout the west. Everybody knows that the situation is critical and will not simply go away. There is general awareness that our society must undergo rapid and fundamental change if we are to survive: sustainable development is the new catch-phrase.

Information technology will play a crucial role in this period of change. This process has already begun: remote sensing and space technology have provided us with graphic images of our beautiful, fragile blue-green planet. Communications and the media have brought news of disasters as they occur, and of positive action, to audiences around the world.

By modelling entities and relationships, database systems provide information repositories which can be tailored to respond to individual queries. Geographic Information System (GIS) computer software extends this concept to model spatial objects and relationships. This technology can speed the process of learning about the world around us. In the right hands, it can facilitate action to protect the environment at all levels, from the local community to international agreements.

Friends of the Earth organizations exist to protect the environment in 47 countries around the world. In the U.K. we have two separate organizations, one for England, Wales and Northern Ireland and another for Scotland. We are independent of government and business; our strength lies in the support of nearly a quarter million U.K. citizens. We have an active campaigning network of over 350 local groups. We campaign at the local, national and international level on a wide range of environmental issues from tropical rainforests, global warming and the ozone layer, through air pollution and acid rain, recycling, waste disposal and renewable energy, to transport and the countryside. Friends of the Earth is ideally positioned to pioneer the use of GIS to support environmental action with accurate and detailed environmental information.

The U.K. government has finally conceded the public's right to know about the quality of our environment. The 1990 Environmental Protection Act, for instance, provides for public access to detailed results of monitoring the emissions to air and water from specific scheduled processes, which include most polluting activities. Waste Regulatory Authorities, in addition, must maintain registers relating to the disposal of waste. Furthermore, European Community (EC) legislation requires public bodies throughout all EC member states to give public access to the information about the environment which they hold.

But simply making data available means nothing if the information technology — information architecture, hardware, and software — is inadequate to the task. Datasets will be practically useless as long as they are held on information systems which are unfriendly, fragmented and unreliable.

In the case of Europe-wide data, the European Environmental Agency (EEA) will serve as a clearinghouse, and could set standards for data quality, interchange and access. However, the establishment of the EEA is being delayed for political reasons and, in the meantime, campaigning organizations like Friends of the Earth can step into the breach.

Because of its ability to integrate many kinds of data on a common spatial base, GIS is a key technology for managing environmental information. GIS is set to become the backbone of information technology within Friends of the Earth, and is foreseen as a key area of growth over the next three years.

We first dabbled with GIS techniques in 1990 by adapting a route planning package to accept data on waste disposal sites. The product of this early experiment was a series of maps showing the locations of waste tips which government consultants had previously identified as posing a threat of water pollution. The maps were reproduced in *The Observer Magazine* in February 1990 and led to nation-wide press coverage and questions in the House of Commons. The results, in campaign terms, were a complete success. The issue of polluting waste tips had been placed firmly on the political agenda. But the effect at a local level was even more startling. *The Observer Magazine* article included a coupon to send back to us for a map showing tips in the reader's locality. By examining the enquirer's postcode, we could quickly identify the appropriate map and mail it out with accompanying information. Such was the efficiency of the system that we answered over 10,000 requests for local maps within two weeks. The system we developed had served its purpose well, but we could foresee a multitude of applications for which we would need a much more powerful tool.

Early last year we began to establish a full-blown GIS. The system uses ESRI's Arc/Info and ArcView software with an SQL RDBNS on a UNIX computing network. We are adopting a long-term and rigorous approach to database construction. Unable to afford Ordnance Survey's prohibitive pricing, we opted for a commercially available 1:250,000 scale Great Britain database. To this we have added designated natural areas and administrative boundaries for England and Wales from the Department of the Environment. On to this topographic and cultural base we are building a database of environmental quality, pollution and potential threats to the environment. The first major data acquisition task has been the loading of the surface water quality archive of the National Rivers Authority: some four million readings for 1990 alone. This has been analysed for breaches of European Community directives on Dangerous Substances and Freshwater Fisheries and results published in the national media. We will load further data sets as they become publicly available.

In tandem with these large-scale data acquisition programs, we are continually loading smaller datasets to a timetable determined by our day-to-day campaigning work. Typically, our campaigners require a map to support a press release on their new research, and the data uploaded is then maintained as a table or coverage in the GIS database. To date we have loaded information on renewable energy developments, toxic tips, and drinking water quality. These are just the first layers; the database will grow steadily over time. Such a database would quickly become unwieldy if not properly managed. For this reason we are paying special attention to the maintenance of metadata concerning data source and quality, as well as access and publication restrictions.

All maps and analyses to date have been produced directly by our two-person GIS team: Rob Atkinson and myself. But considerable effort has also gone into developing a system accessible to occasional and novice users. This capability has been available to campaign staff within our head office since 1992. For terminals we are using 80486 personal computers accessing DOS and Unix applications through an integrated MS-Windows/X-Windows interface. Users are provided with a set of sophisticated yet easy-to-use tools for data management, GIS query and display, and map publication. This suite has been built by linking ESRI's ArcView with applications developed in Arc/Info 6.0 AML, database 4GL and C. The second phase of development will see the addition of map digitizing facilities, the loading of a world dataset and the provision of some GIS analysis capabilities.

Later we will embark on the third, and most exciting, phase of development: providing GIS capacity to our active supporter base throughout England, Wales and Northern Ireland. This is where the real promise of GIS can be fulfilled: in the empowerment of local communities with accurate local environmental information. If information is power, then this means revolution! We will be looking into the feasibility of remote personal computer access to our GIS by dial-up modem. A number of our local groups are already using the international electronic mail and conference network, Green-Net. It would be a logical extension to provide facilities for data upload, GIS textual query and map request by modem.

Ultimately we wish to see a distributed GIS network throughout our organization, at the local, regional, national, and international levels, with appropriate connections to other organizations and databases. An efficient and democratic flow of information is a crucial prerequisite to realize that old ecological maxim: think globally, act locally.

More information on FOE's GIS activities is available from: GIS Manager, Friends of the Earth, 26-28 Underwood St., London N1 7JQ, U.K. Jonathan Doig now lives in Sydney and can be reached at 5/34 Morwick Street, Strathfield, NSW 2135, Australia.

4

New Terrain:
Current Mapping Thought

Introduction

Doug Aberley

Mapping has become such an important part of a widespread process of social and political evolution that there is lively interchange about a host of map-related issues. This is no obtuse dialogue between egghead scientists or isolated academics, but ongoing grassroots discussion and exploration which help mapping to be further evolved as a useful and powerful tool of societal transformation. It is proper that these frontiers be openly explained for all to understand, both as inspiration, and to emphasize (again) the point that we all can participate in deciding along which lines our brave new/old world is drawn. This chapter, then, surveys the current thinking and discussion that is moving the frontier of mapping ever forward.

Talk amongst those who make maps is often predictable. First there is mutual appreciation of a map as something more than a two-dimensional image. Cartographers will usually have a number of favorite images that they can list, and it is not unusual for such folk to have several examples always within reach. Awe of the emotive power of a map is matched by interest in the technical steps that allow the images to be made: the exciting terrain where intent is actualized into the production of an artifact. Stuart Allan, a master cartographer, communicates both the wonder and practical demands of this journey in his article, "Coming to Cartography."

Perhaps the most enduring discussion amongst bioregionalists revolves around the question, "Where is my bioregion?" and "How does it nest with other bioregions into a global interconnection?" Many nights have been extinguished in the search for a single methodology that could answer these questions. There seem to be two schools of thought. Some want people and organizations to define their own bioregions, no matter that borders may overlap. The idea is that once these territories are conceived, informed discussion will eventually merge borders into a biocultural logic. The other school searches for a system that will allow bioregions to be drawn in universal order. Instead of having to conceptualize new territories, reinhabitants would simply look to a single source to see which bioregion they lived in. No doubt it will be a mix of these approaches that will emerge as most useful. Gene Marshall, Seth Zuckerman, and David McCloskey present their preferences.

Finally, there is increasing thought about how mapping can relate to sustainability, preservation of biodiversity, and reclaiming of "the commons." Beyond the use of maps to solve rear-guard land use disputes, this is mapping as the center of a struggle to reclaim an interconnected web of wild ecosystems. On the frontier of this work is a technique called "gap analysis" which was pioneered in the United States and is now figuring prominently in the province-wide land use designation process currently underway in British Columbia. As explained by Earthlife Canada in the *B.C. Gap Analysis Newsletter*, the technique is based on the use of layered GIS images to answer four broad questions:

1. What are the components of natural diversity that require protection?

2. Which of those components are already protected by a protected area system?

3. Which of these areas are not currently protected?

4. What are the best candidate areas for including those unprotected components in the protected area system?

Use of the gap analysis technique is a component of The Wildlands Project initiated by The Cenozoic Foundation, organized by Dave Foreman, and centered in Tucson, Arizona. In a 1992 special issue of the Foundation's excellent periodical *Wild Earth*, a program to aggressively identify and tie together vestiges of the remaining wild land in North America is eloquently spelled out. This is bioregionalism at its practical best: perception of netlike patterns of wildness that begin to define where humans should best nurture settlements and sustainable economic activity. George Tukel explores this frontier where theory and practice meet, linking the making of maps with an introduction to what is the topic of a future Bioregional Series volume: ecological planning.

Although a real *pot pourri*, this chapter is a fair representation of the type of thoughtful purpose that leads us into territories rich in wholistic perception and practical alternatives to an unsustainable status quo.

Coming to Cartography

Stuart Allan

Smitten by the beauty of maps, Stuart Allen pursued his love in graduate school and then worked on the Atlas of Oregon project in 1974. He has been making maps ever since with a company — Raven Maps and Images — that has become dear to the hearts of map afficionados throughout North America. Here he gives a glimpse of the attraction of the business from a professional map-maker's point of view.

An enormous relief map of California used to hang in the Ferry Building in San Francisco. It fascinated me as a kid. And in 1949 a huge "sand table map" of the Sacramento Valley was on display for the opening of the Central Valley Project, in Sacramento, I think. I was entranced, spending the whole afternoon hoping they were going to throw it away and that, somehow, we could take it home. It was probably twenty feet long.

But it never occurred to me to actually make maps, although from our house in the Berkeley hills the view of San Francisco Bay was essentially aerial, and my sister and I both drew that view. A third plaster relief map was directly responsible for me starting graduate school in geography. I was in search of a men's room when I came around a corner and was transfixed by a plaster raised-relief map of Oregon on a wall. After ten minutes of immersion (in a state of elevated consciousness at the time), I decided it was time to enroll in a graduate program which offered the chance to be around such beautiful stuff. But even then it was only very slowly that it dawned on me in a practical, not theoretical, sense that maps were actually made, and that, inasmuch as I enjoyed the drafting and design aspect of the cartography course that all geography students take, I could make them too.

I had at that moment the great luck to fall into a job working on the

State Atlas of Oregon, which gave me an enormous amount of practical experience in the mechanics of making small maps. This was invaluable experience at the time. Now it is possible to make maps entirely on computer, and consequently to become proficient without serving an apprenticeship on a big project. Regardless, there's no substitute for making a lot of maps, of course; if the maps are modest in scope — they can still be beautiful — then the technical requirements can be very limited. Anyone can make maps, just as anyone can whistle, but it still helps to practice a lot.

It seems odd, in retrospect, that maps seemed so compelling but not a thing one could turn one's hand to. This may be the restrictive influence of an excessively book-oriented education? There's also the intractable physical reality of the map, and its daunting technical requirements. After all, anyone can type an essay or record a lab experiment, and the result can look OK, whatever the failing of thought/expression/method in the actual work. But a map sits out there; it is uncompromising in its presence and merciless in its presentation of every failing. That's daunting! And perhaps most importantly, the map, probably because it is such a physical expression, gets believed, gets accepted as a given reality — a credence that is not so readily extended to assembled words on paper. And if the map represents reality, and not just an opinion or a selected/personal version of the truth, then it takes an overweening confidence to just create one. This is an outlook rooted in a misunderstanding or a misperception, in a response to the map as reified truth. But you get over it. And its lingering remnants give a stimulating thrill to the map creation process; you find yourself saying, as the map emerges, "Wow, look at that, the world as I see it!"

A couple of thoughts on the nature of map design are warranted. First, the critical virtue is always clarity. It's the easiest thing to lose, and it will be lost if the map-building is approached in a linear way, with a committee's list of items for inclusion and, further, a committee's political unwillingness to rank these items hierarchically, in terms of importance. Someone has to choose.

Second, maps of any great complexity — virtually any maps in color — are not drawn or painted, they are built. The building process is quite similar to that in cabinet making, or in construction. Get the thing planned out first; it all comes together one step at a time. All the pieces come in sequence, separately, and commonly don't come together, until late in the game. If you save money by combining distinct elements on to a single layer, you foreclose any later opportunity to differentiate them, and that often costs more in effectiveness than was saved in money.

Nearly everyone tries to put too much on a map, and a wonderfully simple corrective to that is to enlarge your base map, or even your completed map. Now that the same information has a lot more room, the eye can manage. This practice is officially taboo for a good but misplaced reason: that enlarging the map doesn't increase accuracy, it increases (perceived) generalization, which is, in a sense, error, and which therefore ought to be minimized. But the point of the map in the end is communication, and a big picture generally communicates more clearly.

The most important thing of all in designing maps that work is to remember always that they are pictures. If they can't be viewed as pictures they are failing. Of course they are pictures of a particular sort, on which distance relationships are always correct within the system of projection which applies, in which consistency and accuracy must take priority, and in which invention of information — not of technique! — has no place. But they're pictures nonetheless.

The distinctive approach we've used in our business at Raven Maps is not in any way new. It simply applies elevation tinting to existing topographic contours, a technique well established two or three generations ago. The Raven execution is unusually detailed, but that has turned out to work very well, in fact, to illustrate the power of a clearly pictorial approach. Complex topographic contours are often very difficult to read; the user must painfully assemble information. Replacing the tangle of lines with a progression of colors makes landforms at once obvious. And as far as possible, what a map presents always should be obvious.

The response to the Raven maps has been gratifying; we hear frequently from people who identify themselves as map lovers, or, not uncommonly, as "closet map freaks." The business was based on the premise that there existed a large community of map lovers and users (and that proved to be true); finding these people was the trick. In Europe there are lots of map dealers, but in North America not so many, and very few bookstores willing or able to take on large sheets. This is unfortunately because the step which makes maps easy to ship and store — folding — is also the one which goes a long way toward wrecking them as visual images. There was also a reluctance on the part of retailers to take on a map selling for $20; the conventional wisdom was that maps should sell for $8 tops. Only a few retailers responded to our deadpan suggestion that they think of these as cheap posters instead of expensive maps. So direct mail sales through a steadily expanding catalogue has been the heart of the business. This has been an educational process for a cartographer who grumps, along with everyone else, about the junk mail in the mailbox; for to someone who doesn't like maps, our catalogue is junk mail. I can find no way out of this, but it is some solace that we send out only a few mailings a year, and that the catalogue itself is small. Our experience also illustrates the drastic changes in retailing/consumption which followed the linked progression of digital processing, delivery services, and credit card purchasing. We happen to operate out of Medford, a town of 50,000 in southwest Oregon; but we could be operating from anywhere.

Raven Maps and Images sell a variety of unique and beautiful maps of North America. They can be reached at 34 N. Central Avenue, Medford, Oregon 97501, U.S.A.

Step One: Mapping the Biosphere

Gene Marshall

Defining your bioregion is often a task that, like peeling an onion, reveals more and more layers before you get to the heart of the matter. Gene Marshall, who has been active in the bioregional movement on local and continental levels for many years, gives an idea of the attractive complexity of bioregional mapping.

L et us just meditate for a moment on the chaos of geographical "districts" we are asked to work with in contemporary society. First of all, in the United States we have the nation as a whole, states, counties and city limits. On top of these, we have state legislative districts, national congressional districts, judicial districts, and perhaps city districts. We have postal zip-code districts and telephone area-code districts and water control districts, and on and on. Few, if any of us, are clear about the boundaries of all these districts. They nevertheless chart and shape our lives. Some of them are gerrymandered and re-gerrymandered into ridiculous patterns. Most of them are personally meaningless to us.

We are usually told by our parents, schools, politicians and television sets to have patriotic feelings for our nation, but what does that actually mean? Certainly, I relate to some of the geography of the United States more passionately than to any part of Canada or Mexico. Part of U.S. geography is familiar to me and has the emotional power of being my home. Yet, Hawaii and Alaska are farther from my "home" experience than Canada or Mexico. Some of my dear friends are Canadian and Mexican citizens. Some of my worst enemies are U.S. citizens. Why must I be willing to go to war for the U.S., fight for U.S. industrial success, and shout loudly for athletic teams that hail from a U.S. place? Why is my home defined by the boundaries of the United States?

I also live within another arbitrarily drawn set of boundaries called "Texas." State patriotism is emphasized here, but I don't actually relate to people living in Houston and El Paso more closely than I do to the people in Oklahoma, only ten miles from where I live. I certainly feel no less at home when I cross the Oklahoma border. It is clear to me that our customary geographical sensibilities and loyalties are in a fuzzy chaos of fragmentary and shallow meanings.

Furthermore, the basic philosophy behind the determination of this maze of geographical districts is antithetical to the society I am envisioning for the future. These "districts" have been set with narrow human purposes in mind: human property rights, human exploitation rights, human political control, human supervision of nature and other humans — these are the motifs that underlie our continued use of these districts.

If we shift our overall imagination from controlling nature to cooperating with nature, other modes of drawing our geographical districts emerge. Recognizing this has been a central gift of the bioregional movement. Efforts have been made in this movement to notice how the planet and all its species of life have already arranged themselves before humans superimposed their districts. Some of the astronauts, speaking in favor of peace, commented that national borders cannot be seen from outer space. Truly that is a basic insight: the biosphere is one interconnected whole. Suppose we begin to look for contiguous parts of this whole: parts whose boundaries are determined by common features of climate, vegetation, fauna, soils, altitude and other geological features. Nature-bonding tribes of humans arranged themselves in harmony with these natural features. Clearly, modern civilizations have ignored them to the point of destroying not only the outward riches of nature itself, but also the meaningfulness of nature-relationships for human beings.

Mapping the biosphere can be a first step, then, in strategic practice because it concretely embodies a crucial shift in our sensibilities from human-centered to nature-centered evaluations in our overall attitude toward nature — a shift from competition to cooperation, from conflict to harmony, from separation to partnership. It is also a meditative exercise that can be done now by each aware person. Agreeing with other aware persons about your proposed geographical boundaries may take years of working together. That does not matter. My need *now* is for my own "sense of place" which depends not simply on discovering my own neighborhood, community or local region, but upon seeing the relationship of my own local places to every other place on the planet. I need a sense of my whole planet, of my continent, and the major sub-parts of my continent in order to see how my local places are parts of these wider regions of natural life and human living.

Some day our political institutions and our economic institutions need to be brought into line with our new geographical sensibilities. But that is not the first step; it comes much later. We have to look forward to at least several decades of transition time during which we will have to live in two worlds: (1) the present political world of nations and states and counties (and other such districts) constructed to define who can exploit what part of the planet, and (2) the coming political world of federated life-regions. Mapping the biosphere is a preparation for that coming day; nevertheless, for right now, as an exercise it enables each individual person to act upon that grand long-range vision. It is also a deeply spiritual act that goes to the heart of our attitudes and values. The way we conceive our geography expresses who we are and defines how we are assuming responsibility for all that surrounds us. This deeply personal level of mapping has primary importance. We cannot turn our mapping task to some professional geographer. Maps which are super-imposed upon us from "higher authorities" or "scientific theorists" mean nothing to us personally unless data from such sources resonate with our personally-felt sense of place.

So step one is a challenge to the individual person to discover a fresh sense of place. This seemingly innocent shift in individual imagination is a radical, revolutionary step. It leads to a demystification of our deeply-embedded national mythologies. When life-regions become "my home," the nation immediately ceases to be "my home" and becomes instead a set of institutions. Speaking as a U.S. citizen, the U.S. ceases to be "my home" and becomes a network of institutions centered in Washington, D.C. and fanning out to 50 state capitals and thousands of county seats. The U.S. is also various "federal" institutions accountable directly to Washington D.C. and scattered across all 50 states and the whole world. This maze of institutions is the United States. I have to live with them and deal with them; they are part of where I live. But once I have made my interior shift in imagination, these U.S. institutions are no longer mythologized for me as "my home." Please listen to the feel of this very carefully: *the United States is no longer my home*. The United States no longer means to me "a people" or "a home" of any sort for anyone. The United States, on this side of "Mapping the Biosphere," is simply a maze of institutions.

So, looking with fresh eyes from this new sense of home, I can observe the U.S. maze of institutions objectively. Are any of them any good for anything? Can any of them be used to do good? Are some them capable of being phased out right away? Are some of them capable of being transformed into something useful that lasts a thousand years? Are some of them useful for the next hundred years of transition and then disposable? Once we have mapped the biosphere, our responses to such questions can be rendered in a simple, practical manner, unpolluted by the national mythologies we have been trained in since infancy.

The essential simplicity of visualizing a new sense of place can be illustrated by a ritual that I have conducted as part of a number of speeches. I ask the audience to stand up, imagine that they are standing, right below their feet, on their county, on the state of Texas, on the nation of the United States. "Now we are going to leap in the air, leaping out of this county, out of Texas, out of United States. When we come back down to the ground we are going to land on this bioregion, on this continent, on this planet. With this leap you have begun the complex task of reinhabiting the planet; you have joined the bioregional movement."

This leap needs some fleshing out. What exactly *is* my bioregion? How is it related to my continent? What do we mean by communities and neighborhoods, and which ones comprise my bioregion? So, still focusing on a shift in the imagination of the individual person, I want to expand upon this shift. I want to challenge each individual leaper to do some mapping. This challenge is summarized in the accompanying chart which you can adopt for your own use:

General Geographic Categories	My Own Examples
My Neighborhood	Timber Creek Watershed
My Community	Bois d'Arc Creek Watershed
My Local Bioregion	Red River Flats
My Sub-Biome	Southern Great Prairie
My Biome	The Great Prairie
My Continent	Turtle Island
My Planet	Earth

The number and names of categories along the left side of the chart can be changed. The definitions of these geographical scales can be altered. However, for me, this is a good chart and a place to begin. I will explain more carefully what each of these categories mean to me:

My Neighborhood means the most local place in which I live. It could be a few square miles; it could be a few square blocks. It could contain 200 people in a rural valley or a small creek watershed; it could contain 500-1,000 people in a very small urban space.

My Community is larger: 5,000 to 20,000 people may live there. Again, rural places will be less populous, urban places may be more populous. Community, as well as neighborhood, does not mean humans only, but rocks and water and vegetation and all local forms of animal life. Some communities are now vastly overpopulated with human beings. A community in an urban setting would likely be small enough to walk easily to every part of it. A more rural community might be larger, like most of a county.

My Local Bioregion is a collection of communities within some meaningful boundaries determined by the factors of basic land topography, watersheds, flora and fauna habitats, altitudes, rainfalls, temperatures, and other such factors.

One of the important human factors defining a local bioregion is the principle that it should be large enough to be relatively self-sustaining. A community or a neighborhood may be quite dependent on other communities and neighborhoods for many of the necessities and cultural enrichments of life. A local bioregion may also have imports and exports of all sorts to and from all parts of the planet; nevertheless, a local region, when fully transformed in the next millennium, should be able to be relatively capable of feeding itself, caring for its own natural systems, clothing and housing its humans, living a full, well-rounded life with minimal dependence on other regions.

My Sub-Biome means the next larger life-region. It is a nesting together of perhaps 20 local bioregions. My local bioregion is about 100 miles north to south and 120 miles east to west, whereas my sub-biome, it seems to me, extends from the northern border of Red River watershed to the Gulf of Mexico on the south, and the western and eastern borders are determined by the borders of that banana-shaped strip of grasslands which extends from Canada to the Gulf of Mexico.

My Biome is that entire grasslands which I am calling The Great Prairie. The term "biome" I have taken from the excellent mapping work done by a United Nations office (the Man And the Biosphere Secretariat, Division of Ecological Sciences, UNESCO) which produced a map of all the large natural regions of the planet that they called biomes. This map has a degree of acceptance across the world and is, at least, a good way for each of us begin our life-long task of defining what large sub-part of our continent we live within.

My Continent is quite clear to me. I see myself living on what some call North America, but I am using the name "Turtle Island" in honor of this continent's ancient residents. In my definition of it, this continent includes Costa Rica but not Panama; Alaska but not Asia; Greenland but not Iceland; and the northernmost Caribbean Islands. Clearly these decisions are somewhat arbitrary and other persons on Turtle Island may decide differently about what Turtle Island includes. Nevertheless, this is my map, remember — my meditation on where I live.

My Planet is the clearest category of all. I simply mean the entire biosphere, its undergirding rock and metal ball, and its surrounding atmosphere.

These geographical delineations are important to me because they chart my circles of responsibility. It is as if I am standing in the center of several concentric circles. Immediately around me is my own domestic home, the next larger circle is my neighborhood, and so on, out to the largest circle, my planet. The full meaning of the word "home" is all these circles. I stand at one point in space which is inside all these circles. Choosing clearly what each of these circles includes enables me to explain to myself where I am and how to focus the various aspects of my work. Take my sub-biome, for example. I am actively related to activities throughout this geographical scope. Though I know people throughout the continent and the planet, I work most frequently with people in my sub-biome. I identify with this larger home in some important ways. I assume responsibility for this area in ways I do not assume responsibility for any other "sub-biome" on the planet. While I am convinced that I must now focus my energies on empowering my own neighborhood and community, I also feel responsible for inspiring and aiding every neighborhood and community in my sub-biome. I meet quarterly with people from two or three adjacent bioregions in my sub-biome. When we come together, we see ourselves as a group of servant-leaders who return home to various neighborhoods and communities where we devote ourselves to planning and creating local empowerment.

Mapping the biosphere charts your identity with, and responsibility for, the whole Earth of which you are one glorious part. It is the first step toward shifting the center of political gravity from the nation and its moneyed élites to more local circles of responsibility.

◆

Four Reasons Why You've Never Seen a Map of the Northern California Bioregion

Seth Zuckerman

The particular way in which you look at your bioregion defines the way you describe it. Seth Zuckerman, who lives in northern California's Mattole Valley, and writes on the relations between people and the rest of the natural world, succintly makes the point.

Whether we call it "Shasta," "Alta California," or simply "here," we who live in northern California have been identifying our-selves for years with a territory that is larger than our own riverine watersheds but smaller that the Pacific Slope or the State of California. The boundaries of this region have never been clear, although everyone agrees that Los Angeles lies outside of them. Here's how it looks to draw the line four dif-ferent ways.

(1) Snow that falls on Mt. Shasta eventually finds its way to the ocean through San Fran-cisco Bay and the Golden Gate. This map of the watershed to which most of Shasta belongs — the Sacramento-San Joaquin — does justice to the story of northern California waters, but enforces separations that cleave through continui-ties of vegetation and soil, such as the Klamath-Sacramento divide or the ridgeline between the upper Eel and Clear Lake/Cache Creek. It also lumps the Pit watershed with the rest of Shasta, even though its basin shares more plants and geological heritage with eastern Oregon's dry steppes than with Sierran mixed conifer forest or bayside salt marsh.

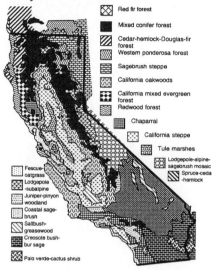

Red fir forest

Mixed conifer forest

Cedar-hemlock-Douglas-fir forest
Western ponderosa forest

Sagebrush steppe

California oakwoods

California mixed evergreen forest
Redwood forest

Chaparral

California steppe

Tule marshes

Lodgepole-alpine-sagebrush mosaic
Spruce-cedar-hemlock

Fescue-oatgrass
Lodgepole-subalpine
Juniper-pinyon woodland
Coastal sage-brush
Saltbush-greasewood
Creosote bush-bur sage
Palo verde-cactus shrub

(2) A site's vegetation reflects the panoply of influences on that location, from soil to climate. So it might be natural to look at plant life as an indicator of bioregional boundaries. But how to interpret the tortured configuration of vegetation types in and around northern California? Geographers identify some 15 vegetation types within the presumptive borders of our region. One association, the cedar-hemlock-Douglas fir forest, parallels the redwood belt for 150 miles, then extends north past Puget Sound. The saltbush-greasewood scrub community can be found in the San Joaquin Valley —

and in Nevada, Idaho and eastern Oregon. Meanwhile, what forges a coherent whole from the chaparral and bunchgrass, red fir and oak woodland?

(3) Among 21 major language groups and 500 tribal groups of native California, anthropologists distinguish a "California culture area" based on patterns of subsistence (reliance on the acorn) as well as the architecture of dwellings and beliefs. The Yurok, Karok, Hupa and Wiyot

Chetco
Klamath
NW
Lutuami
Calif.
Modoc
Karok
Yurok
Achomawi
Wiyot

Central California

NW Calif. : Culture provinces

Pomo: Language and tribal groups

Pomo
Maidu

Patwin

Miwok

Costanoan
Yokuts
Salinan
Great Basin

Serrano
Chumash Southern California
Cahuilla
Luiseno

are classed with peoples to the north, because of their plank-houses, world renewal dances, and relation to the salmon. To the south, the influence of Pueblo culture appears; to the east lies the Great Basin and its peoples who could not rely on the material abundance of the California lifeplace.

(4) Topography, parent material and geologic history — these basic elements of terrain are the stuff of which geomorphic provinces are made. This map provides a neat southern and eastern boundary to our region, at the edge of the Transverse Ranges, Mojave Desert and Great Basin. As always, the north end is problematic: if we embrace Mt. Lassen and Mt. Shasta itself, which are part of the Cascade volcanic chain, what will stop us before we reach Mt. Hood and gaze down upon the Columbia River?

Ask the question, "Where is northern California?" in four different ways, and four different answers emerge. From which we see all of these factors and others such as climate, distribution of totem animals, current patterns of subsistence, soil types, soulful identification will need to be taken into account. The result will be a smorgasbord of maps, many of whose boundaries are soft, not hard, shading from one region to the next. The topic is blessed with enough ambiguity that we can draw lines and erase them, exploring and adapting, laughing and arguing, for decades to come.

Sources: Hydrology: California Department of Forestry, Forest and Rangeland Resources Assessment Program. Vegetation: adapted from A.W. Küchler, Potential Natural Vegetation of the United States, 1964. Native culture: A.L. Kroeber, California Culture Provinces, University of Calif. Publications in American Archaeology and Ethnology, vol. 17, 1920. Physiography: Historical Atlas of California, University of Oklahoma Press, 1981, and William G. Loy et al, Atlas of Oregon, University of Oregon Books, 1976.

◆

On Ecoregional Boundaries

David McCloskey

Boundaries in nature are sometimes clear and distinct but, more often than not, they are fuzzy and controversial. This leads frequently to much debate among bioregionalists about how to come up with satisfactory definitions of natural regions. David McCloskey, a long-time bioregionalist who teaches sociology, anthropology and human ecology at Seattle University, is the author of the map of Cascadia, a region whose natural features incorporate parts of Alaska, British Columbia and Washington.

Imagine a world that makes sense. Mentally erase all the tangled lines on the old, industrial-age maps — city, county, state, and provincial boundaries, highways and railroads, the international borders. Let the original face of the place shine through: rivers, mountains and valleys, coastlines and plateaus, sea and sky. Listen again to the spirits of these places, and pay close attention to what gives them their special character. Learn to tell the story of the place, and ask: How do the maps and models in our heads need to be redrawn in order to help give greater voice to the land itself?

In discerning ecoregional boundaries, we might set out several norms as guidelines.

First, ecoregional boundaries should be natural, not artificial or arbitrary. For an authentic ecoregional boundary is discovered as an emergent out of the land itself and the reflections of the people living in place, rather than being imposed as a "line on a map" by experts in far distant centers, or by global cities for their own special purposes.

Second, "soft" versus "hard" borders are misplaced metaphors; rather the problem is whether the boundaries "speak" or not — whether they are inchoate or articulate. For ecoregional boundaries are neither necessarily soft nor fuzzy; while there are few straight lines in nature, there are many definite and powerful edges — various "ecotones," watershed divides, climatic zones, fault-lines and scarps, and so on. Careful attention should be given to such beginnings and endings, for

The map of Cascadia, originated by
David McCloskey.

these dramatic turnings in the Earth serve as clear and powerful articulations of diversity.

Third, ecoregional boundaries are multiple, not singular, in nature. Rather than focusing on the political level and allowing that to overrule all other considerations, authentic boundaries must, first and foremost, be ecologically and culturally grounded. Now, the key quality of ecoregions is that they stand forth as bounded wholes in space and time (obviously, distinctiveness does not imply isolation). In spatial terms, the life of the land is carried out on many different levels or "planes." Imagine each of the key dimensions — geographical land forms, geologic formations, tectonic imprints, and soil series; climatic zones and seasonal migrations of high and low pressure cells; hydrologic features; botanical and zoological features such as type, number and diversity of species, their geographic and especially seasonal ranges; ecological features such as habitats, landscapes, and biomes; ethnographic maps of native peoples and their migration patterns and current use; and so on — as clear plastic sheets overlaid on a base map of landforms. An ecoregion emerges, then, as a composite whole where the most significant features converge in a distinct and sustained way.

It all requires patient fieldwork, careful attention to telling details and larger patterns, as well as insight and creativity to discern the emergent whole. What "ecoregionalists" are after is the configuration or deep gestalt of parts and wholes, a true matrix in which things are naturally woven together. There's a certain delight in watching a new "figure" emerge from the "field" or background. One spontaneously says, "Aha! That's it!" — as if seeing home for the first time.

As Thomas Berry reminds us (in *Dream of the Earth*), "The Earth presents itself to us not as a uniform global reality but as a complex of highly differentiated regions caught up in the comprehensive unity of the planet itself." Indeed, just as we know the parts of own bodies, so, too, we should learn the parts of that collective, extended body we call "Earth," and how they work together. For the world is a natural integrity, not a willed unity or forced totality. Watersheds, ecoregions, and macro-regions are the prime natural units through which this larger, collective body articulates itself. Today more than ever we need to learn to move step by step, carefully and respectfully through these mediating levels between local and planetary life.

It's the special resonance between these various layers and levels above and below that sets the land to singing, and gives us our working metaphors of wholeness, the rhythms or true measure of place. Remember that it is the emergent life of the place as a whole — cultural as well as biological and physical — that we seek to recognize and represent. This is a new task, one that goes well beyond politics or environmentalism in traditional senses. It is one of the true quests of ecoregionalism.

Fourth, perhaps the crucial factor in distinguishing one ecoregion from another is that the place, species, and peoples have evolved together ("co-evolution"). A shared dynamic unity of formation is the decisive factor in discovering the distinctive character and boundaries of an ecoregion.

Hence, it is essential to note that ecoregional boundaries reveal temporal as well as spatial dimensions. Just as our body has its own rhythms, so, too, lived territory expands and contracts with the rhythms of the day, month, season, and year, and even longer cycles. Rather than being "soft" borders, then, ecoregional boundaries may exhibit a kind of seasonal elasticity; the seasonal migration of climatic cells of the Aleutian low and Hawaiian high, as they move north and south in the north-eastern Pacific Ocean bringing summer and winter weather, are an obvious case in point. The moving border between them up and down the coasts from Baja to Alaska is called "spring" and "fall." Indeed, in the weathers above and the waters below one can never hope to determine fixed boundaries as on land. Salmon migrations, the seasonal migrations of many species of birds and mammals, even the long-term march of the trees north and south, with the glacial ebb and flood, remind us of the elemental nature of temporal rhythms. Ecoregional boundaries therefore take on the special character of a true borderland, a crossing-over-and-back in time as well as space.

In sum, ecoregional boundaries are natural wholistic "emergents." They are found where key levels overlap forming distinctive patterns. Look to the special ways in which the face of the land, tectonic forces below, weather patterns above, the flow of waters, flora and fauna, native peoples, and cultural identities converge and reinforce one another. In emerging from the life of the land as a whole, ecoregional boundaries stand forth as convergent thresholds welcoming us "home."

◆

Wild at the Heart: Planning from the Wild Center Out

George Tukel

The movement to define bioregions and to bring them into active use is perhaps the only way to avoid the massive simplification of ecosystems brought about by ever more intense human encroachment upon wild areas. George Tukel is a bioregional planner who currently works on landscape designs that preserve natural biodiversity while supporting land uses that are regenerative. In this article he puts forward a far-sighted proposal for recreating "the commons" in order to help preserve the diversity of wild species.

Wilderness at the center of regions once again live and well .... Social cooperation woven into the life cycle of natural systems .... A return to beauty and ecological health as guides to community growth .... These could be changes you would feel in your bones —

transforming the regional landscape by exchanging industrial sources of guides for living for wild ones.

But that means tricky currents to navigate. Realistically, to get there, we must shift our point of reference to wilderness as Thoreau described it: as a landscape of sacred places, as home to native species and entire biotic communities, as the teacher of enduring ethics. But to make this choice, we have to be prepared to say goodbye to the city as the center of the world.

This present and dominant landscape pattern, the result of autonomous regions becoming "functional urban" areas, is by now familiar. The decaying city center gives way to the suburbs, suburban crawl pushes into the countryside, picturesque countryside ends at the edge of parkland designed as a refuge for the stresses of city living. So endemic is this urban-based configuration to our everyday view of regions that both reformers and defenders take its existence for granted. There might be fervent argument over whether growth or "greening" should be given higher priority, but the specific context of place for this debate remains a constant: the city-centered regional landscape.

Changing from an urban to a wild region is within our grasp, but we're not going to get there by simply amending a few zoning laws to mask the effects of urbanization. Drawing upon the wilderness that remains, we need choices that aren't disguises for city-centered industrial expansion. In looking at a viable alternative, my north star is the anciently charted territory of a wild regionalism, which has been redrawn in the United Nations-originated notion of Biosphere Reserves.

In the late '60s and early '70s, conservationists and land managers reacted to development pressures that threatened natural diversity within large national parks by struggling to articulate a coevolutionary use of preserved areas. They had realized that the survival of biodiversity within parks depended on human land use reform and restoration of ecosystems outside of them. And they understood that thriving natural systems could provide the information required for such ecodevelopment. This interrelationship between subsistence economies and natural systems came to be expressed in the Biosphere Reserve model. The power of the biosphere model lies in the dialogue it opens between the non-human world and people who want to bypass the poverty and ruin of industrialization. This communication guides human land use and invigorates wilderness because the principles of biodiversity lay the groundwork for sustainable development. The emphasis on sustainability reduces the shock to natural systems. Natural systems in turn point the way for restoration, and restoration brings the

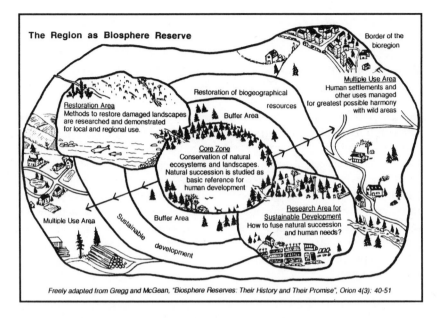

The Region as Biosphere Reserve

Border of the bioregion

Multiple Use Area
Human settlements and
other uses managed
for greatest possible harmony
with wild areas

Restoration of biogeographical resources

Restoration Area
Methods to restore damaged landscapes
are researched and demonstrated
for local and regional use.

Buffer Area

Core Zone
Conservation of natural
ecosystems and landscapes.
Natural succession is studied as
basic reference for
human development

Multiple Use Area

Sustainable development

Buffer Area

Research Area for
Sustainable Development
How to fuse natural succession
and human needs?

Freely adapted from Gregg and McGean, "Biosphere Reserves: Their History and Their Promise", Orion 4(3): 40-51

system full circle by enhancing biological richness. Good talk among species respectful of one another.

The basic building block of the Biosphere Reserve is the core zone of wilderness: the protected regional place where natural diversity survives. Core areas differ radically from usual land preservation efforts, which tend toward single species or scenery. Instead, core areas conserve multiple vegetation types and species within intact and representative ecosystems. Surrounding this wild heartland is a buffer area, and beyond the buffer area multiple land uses are allowed which provide for human needs but are based on natural characteristics of the core zone.

For those who understand the worth of perennial resources, the Biosphere Reserve is well suited as a starting point for transforming urban regions into bioregions — where wild systems supplant the city as the center. But the model wasn't really created for more developed areas because it assumes large available natural areas to build core zones around, such as national parks. If we want to adapt the Biosphere Reserve model to built up North American regions, we need to compensate for the urbanized condition of landscapes that most of us live with every day, in which there remain only fragments of native ecosystems. And we can do that by modifying the concept to include smaller patches of wilderness and by introducing natural corridors as bridges between them.

Wild core zones of bioregions don't require just one huge area to be alive enough to maintain diversity, even though that might be ideal. Instead, there could also be clusters of smaller core zones, a choice that becomes especially important given the pervasive distribution of human populations, which have cut up wild areas and left few intact. Still, the islands of wilderness, no matter how strengthened by diversity and buffer zones, will simplify towards extinction over time if they are not connected by land to each other. Natural corridors could span them, say with bands running along, and including, waterways.

Natural corridors, though, should not be confused with the current popular concept of greenways, which usually are recreational corridors linking human communities with open spaces. Greenways, such as hiking trails and bike paths that have replaced many old railway lines, aren't adequate to the ecological task at hand. More important for wildness, especially in deeply disturbed terrain, are wide swaths of land that are ecological extensions of core areas and that establish connection between them.

Corridors are a key to the long term health of the region because these ecological connections allow natural diversity within the cores to flourish. Balancing for the lack of core land mass with broad corridors could open breathing space for plant communities and watershed processes to invigorate themselves. Corridors could keep invasive exotics at bay helping the more fragile interior species to survive. And larger animals would roam further afield without running into paved or clearcut human places. While large wilderness preserves should be established wherever possible, cores and corridors will be the practical solution for realizing the goals of the Biosphere Reserve in regions where industrialization has left its mark.

RECREATING THE COMMONS

Together with its biological value, a regionalism built on biodiversity can reestablish the primacy of the commons, that ancient voice of community where social well-being is undivided from the care and freedom given to the shared world of natural worth. In older times, common land managed according to local customs and experience of natural events was the foundation for ongoing sustenance, along with efforts on private property. The commons also acted as community glue for cooperative efforts. The everyday evidence that sustained yield land practices work to the benefit of all was there to see and trust in.

In caring for the commons, the community as a whole was forced to address key questions, determining its identity in the process. What are the responsibilities of land use when resources are shared? What to let be, what land to work, and how to enrich the soil? How to house and clothe so that fish return and the water is clear? The commons, because it was land and resources necessary to individual and group survival, became a local social institution for answering these questions. Neither private property nor public lands, the commons represents a third type of land ownership where conviviality and natural diversity are not luxuries but requirements of communities. Cores and corridors can become the commons of the bioregion, offering land and the tradition for healing both wildness and human communities.

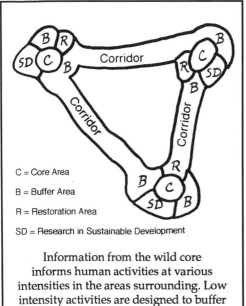

C = Core Area

B = Buffer Area

R = Restoration Area

SD = Research in Sustainable Development

Information from the wild core informs human activities at various intensities in the areas surrounding. Low intensity activities are designed to buffer core and corridor.

The Biosphere Reserve offers the opportunity to reconceive land ownership and preservation with the recovery of the commons. But, in practice, if we concentrate only on the preservation of biodiversity (and it's easy to do with native landscapes and species rapidly disappearing around us) without creative efforts at human land use, then we'll be ignoring the reasons why the Biosphere Reserves were envisioned in the first place. We need equal attention paid to human extensions of wilderness—sustainability, for example—understanding that what we do outside the cores and corridors is as essential to the richness of habitats as the cores and corridors themselves.

But, finally, with the modified Biosphere Reserve model, sustainable activities would have the surround necessary for their success. Cores and corridors would provide instruction and everyday sensual support for land uses like organic farming and sustainable forestry. Where now these efforts seem like anachronisms within the city-dominated region, they would nestle easily into landscapes ripe with diversity. Farms would share borders and productivity with corridors, and forestry practices would mimic old growth core areas.

Hand-in-hand with climax sustainable development, restoration of natural systems could begin that travels from city edge to the wild insides of the bioregion and back again with natural succession providing the trailmarkers.

Restoration, as cultural practice and technic, shares much with good farming. Outside and inside the circle of life, restoration work rests on careful observation and works best when technique is fused to climax information from wild areas, when diversity flourishes while human needs are satisfied.

Restorationists would play an unusually important role in the bioregion. For starters, they could be working to recover and build up into core areas the remnants of wild systems, probably with the urbanized green areas and larger parks. Old growth and complex water places that include floodplains, wetlands and seasonal streams — rich species and plant habitats — come quickly to mind. Many restorationists would also become biocentric land use consultants, designing corridors in addition to providing the nuts and bolts guidance for, say, the renewal of stream bed and life.

In the end, perhaps, what restorationists will have really accomplished will be more elementary, more in the soul. They will have returned to local culture a trust in the understanding of natural systems for cohesion and reciprocity. When that day comes, a change will have occurred. Our understanding of community will have deepened into shared knowledge and traditions of living in places now beautiful enough to feed both belly and imagination.

A TOOL FOR THE JOB

Consider the possibility: wild regional configurations, with us growing in them. If this is to remain a realistic choice — where ideas of natural diversity provide the guidance for grounding settlement patterns and identity — there will have to be a shift in efforts at land preservation from the present emphasis on creating pleasant pieces of recreational green space, to creating the cores and corridors that can marry wildness to restoration and sustainability. But where to start?

Mapping could kick things off. To different degrees, there are many undisturbed areas which include state, or federal lands, privately-held properties with conservation easements on them, and land trusts. It would be important to identify and map these areas, creating a picture of existing land reserves and future possibilities. A big job. But, in many cases, important information already exists on the locations and specifics of natural systems. Among others, there are directories of wetlands and old growth that broaden out to regional perspectives provided by Geographical Information Systems (GIS).

A GIS is computerized cartography based on creating layers of information — soils, vegetation and land use, for example — and then overlaying them to reveal patterns of the natural and cultural landscape (if you're familiar with Ian McHarg's book, *Design With Nature*, you'll already know the importance of this method for town and watershed planning).

Using the data-handling and image-making power of GIS, combined with local knowledge of watersheds, it's possible to identify core areas for the bioregion, heartlands that include full ranges of ecological conditions and landscapes. We can locate where the later stages of natural succession of all native ecosystems — old growth, or climax — still exist. We know where populations of indicator and endangered species dwell and where habitats associated with species richness lie.

We can map these different areas with GIS and see how they are positioned in relation to each other within the regional landscape. Sometimes they will overlap, sometimes they will be scattered all over, but under any circumstances, we will be seeing the first outlines of core areas. We can then go back to our first map of reserve areas and overlay our map of possible core zones on top of it. The difference between the two maps could be the basis for locally-created work plans for preserving land, building on existing reserves wherever possible, to build up the centers of biodiversity required for regional rejuvenation.

Once the location of core zones is ascertained, we can savvy out the corridors that should span them. Designing the corridors and making them work will be complex. They will require a different type of effort from that of creating core areas which benefit from being visible and large enough to be a clear priority of daily preservation activities. On the other hand, corridors will be molded from many small pieces, crossing the boundary lines of public and private properties and watersheds.

GIS can help this process along. Politically realistic routes for corridors can be mapped by analyzing land ownership on the local and regional levels, tailoring corridors to undeveloped lands under friendly public and private stewardship. The location of highways and roads within the proposed corridors can be plotted and strategies formed to overcome the effect on wildlife of what is probably the severest of habitat fragmenters. Landforms and waterways, vegetation, soils and contours can then be overlaid on to corridor candidates to assure watershed pattern and continuity.

GIS can also help grassroots groups from being stampeded into the

An Ecological Reserve System for the North Coastal Basin – the work of Map Rap. As the present industrial context evolves into a wild one, core territories and corridors would fill out until surveyor's lines gave way to a regional configuration with human settlements appearing as islands surrounded by natural areas rich in diversity.

Humboldt Bay

Cape Mendocino

Pacific Ocean

Point Arena

Allowable annual rates of harvest, as a percentage of inventory:

● 0%   ◕ 0.5– 1.5%   ○ Sustainable harvest

decisions on biodiversity favoured by larger institutions. The updating of maps, while providing the means of new information, is also the occasion for communication between local and regional workers. On the regional level, working across natural borders, local peoples can carry out the reiterative process of refining the overall design of the corridors. And, within borders, the tough questions can be taken on — the design and management of the corridors, and their location and boundary definitions — knowing that there are clear connections to the larger picture. The result? Instead of reacting on the sidelines to decisions made far-off, we will create watershed-based regional alternatives that are alive and native and worth fighting for.

5

How to Map Your Bioregion: A Primer for Community Activists

Doug Aberley

In more and more of the struggles to ensure a sustainable future, citizens' groups are having to present detailed and sophisticated arguments to convince authorities to change their ways. This requires painstaking attention both to gathering data and to presenting it in its most eloquent form. While the broad strokes of the bioregional mapping strategy are perhaps easy enough to grasp, the actual details of the process deserve a full enough treatment to enable ordinary people to start right away on the job. The following primer is the product of the last fifteen years of living and working in Northwest British Columbia as a town planner, regional planner, and municipal administrator, and of a study undertaken at the University of British Columbia that has been shaped and further adapted by many hours of lively debate over maps and bioregions.

The purpose of this guide is to explain a method of identifying and describing bioregions. To show how this method works, a series of maps and graphs will be presented that together demonstrate a technique that may be used to take bioregionalism from a utopian "urge," to a working perception of newly constituted territories. For demonstration purposes, the primer will be completed on a step-by-step basis to define a bioregion that includes Northwest British Columbia. With the help of the written and visual explanations offered, any reinhabitant should be able to easily complete a similar series of exercises for any area of the Earth. The completed atlas that results will be a valuable aid in "learning home," and could also become an organizing tool useful in focusing bioregional intent into action.

71

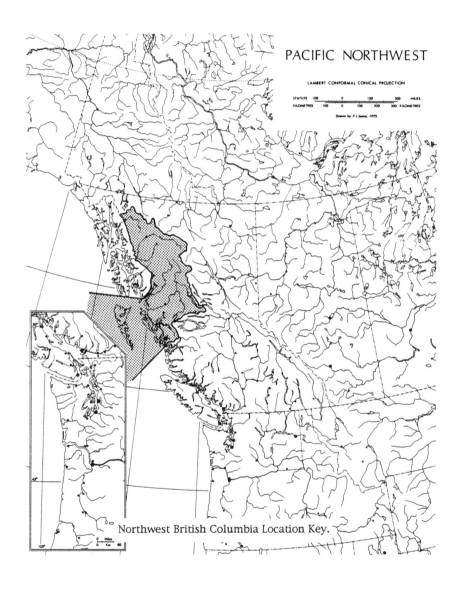

PACIFIC NORTHWEST

LAMBERT CONFORMAL CONICAL PROJECTION

Northwest British Columbia Location Key.

While this primer is mostly a technical document, it should be reiterated that maps hold a magic that is anything but technical. Maps are a human attempt to represent the incredible complexities of time and space. They are shorthand for perceptions that each of us create with senses evolved as hunters and gatherers, as explorers, as animals that must navigate to survive. A map becomes more than a series of lines; it becomes an agenda for action, a turf to defend, a series of memories that remind of action and pleasure and history. Maps have been made that inflame war and hatred; maps have been made that create new visions of human society. It is with great reverence that the maps in this primer were created.

The primer is organized into five sections. The first shows how the *external* boundaries of a bioregion can be identified. The second section then explains ways to describe *territory within* the newly defined bioregion. The third section demonstrates a method of isolating historic and current information about the *economic base* of the bioregion. The fourth section describes how smaller *"local"* areas within bioregions can be described. And finally, a conclusion ties the pieces together. Again, each of these sections uses Northwest British Columbia as a model, showing how the theory of bioregion description can be applied in the context of a specific biocultural region.

This atlas first evolved on dog-eared sheets of paper that were carried on ten years of journeys made through valleys carved by the Skeena, Nass, and Stikine rivers. The maps were occasionally shared with others, but primarily were a personal meditation on the identity of "home." Later they were expanded and used as part of a Masters Thesis completed in 1985 at the University of British Columbia's School of Community and Regional Planning. The thesis, titled "Bioregionalism: A Territorial Approach To Governance and Development of Northwest British Columbia," described the history of the region, how it has been governed and developed by absentee interests, and how bioregionalism might offer a sustainable alternative to the status quo. Maps extracted from the 452-page document have since been annotated and presented at a number of workshops and seminars to explain the use and potential of bioregional mapping. Many comments have been received in this process, and the primer has been amended accordingly. The maps will no doubt continue to evolve, becoming more comprehensive with the addition of further layers of description, the inclusion of an equal level of detail for the Alaska portion of the bioregion, and the development of a method whereby maps and tables could easily be updated as new information is received. By their very nature, bioregion atlases can be amended continuously, mirroring changes in individual and community perception of place.

Due to space limitations, only a portion of the bioregion mapping exercise and accompanying explanation contained in the original study are reproduced here. Every attempt has been made to include at least one example of each type of illustration or other method of displaying bioregion data. Notes are included throughout the primer to properly credit sources, and to help demonstrate the broad range of written and graphic material that can be surveyed in a bioregion mapping process.

◆

Section 1:
External Bioregion Boundaries

A central theme in bioregional literature is that bioregions will somehow describe themselves by organizing and layering information relating to various "natural" systems and communities. This approach is appealing because it side-steps the more traditional straight-line boundaries which characterize the human division of property. Thus, if we overlay watershed information with animal communities, with vegetation types, with physiographic (landform) regions, etc., we will delineate external borders of bioregions. This technique is known as "physiographic determinism," and has been successfully used in progressive regional planning for over fifty years. Excellent examples of how this technique can be applied are included in books titled *Design With Nature* by Ian McHarg, and *The Living Landscape* by Frederick Steiner.

The major dilemma in using strictly natural elements to define bioregions is that there is no easy way to give human scale to the territories defined. Is the entire Pacific drainage of North America a bioregion because this area shares a common westward tilt? Are biogeographical provinces that span tens of degrees of latitude and longitude "home?" Using these type of criteria alone makes it impossible to define bioregions that make sense.

In order to perceive bioregions which will reorient human activity towards dynamic balance in nature, it is necessary to make human occupation of any land area a part of the bioregion definition equation.

The boundary layering process which will be described thus incorporates human elements in order to help focus border definition to a scale which is meaningful to regularly interacting groups of reinhabitant communities. This approach captures the essence of the bioregional ideal: to irrevocably marry human activity into processes of sustainable land, animal, plant, and atmospheric interaction. The goal of this primer is to teach a technique that will allow any reinhabitant to achieve an informed perception of bioregion scope and scale. In the revealing of layers of biocultural fact, natural territorial units will disclose their presence in a way that will make powerful social, economic, and political sense to anyone who lives in that region. When reinhabitants then compare the territories they have discovered, boundaries can be wiggled into rough alignment as consensus is evolved. The primer thus becomes a communication tool that allows bioregion territories to be learned, shared, and then adopted as physical arenas within which sustained transformative action will occur.

What follows is description of a process that will aid any interested person or group in defining the external boundaries of their bioregion. Information required to build the maps and tables is readily accessible, and only demands that basic library research skills be used to ferret region-specific data from diverse sources.

Base Map

You need to find a base map which shows a land area sufficient to "frame" the bioregion you will define. Because this first map is the foundation upon which a whole series of bioregion images will be drawn, the way in which it should be prepared will be explained in some detail.

The first step is to find a public or university library which has collected a large number of maps covering the region you wish to study. Universities are especially good sources of the many types of graphic materials that can make completion of the base map a relatively simple exercise.

Once you have located a map source, beg, borrow or buy the tools you will use to create the base map. You will need a pencil with .05 mm hard leads, 11 by 17 inch or larger tracing paper (10 sheets to start with), a soft eraser, a notebook, and access to a light table (usually available in map libraries or university geography departments).

Arrive early at the map repository and find a table in the area where you are allowed to take any map that you wish to study. Once you are set up, it is a prudent idea to introduce yourself to the librarian on duty and explain what your purpose is. To the people who work with them, maps are almost sacred images, to be protected with a careful vigilance. The time it takes to make a pleasant introduction will allow the librarian to orient you to the library's rules, and possibly gain you a valuable ally who can be of great assistance in locating the information you will need.

Maps are stored in flat files, thin drawers which contain a number of map sheets. Each drawer usually contains a variety of maps which describe a similar category of information for a specific geopolitical territory. For example, a number of flat files will contain maps covering Canada, with individual drawers storing images of hydrology, elevation contours, soils, vegetation, and the like. Your first task is thus to find files which contain relatively uncluttered images of your region at a scale which will allow you to trace a base map.

Maps come in many varieties. For the purposes of this study three types of maps will be most useful: topographic, planimetric, and thematic. Topographic maps show the three-dimensional shape of the land by using imaginary contour lines drawn to connect all points at a similar elevation above or below sea level. Each contour line represents a different elevation. If contour lines are close together, it signals a steep landscape. Contour lines spaced farther apart define a flatter terrain. Planimetric maps show a territory without any reference to contours. Usually, the most dominant features of a planimetric map are rivers, coastlines, lakes, spot elevations, and some human-adapted features such as towns and roads. Thematic maps project specific sets of information on a map base. Maps which show data on Native territories, human population distributions, wildlife ranges, or any other of a countless number of possible representations of point, linear, volume, area, or other data are thus thematic in nature.

Other types of mapping include air or satellite photos of land areas, cadastral maps which show legal ownership patterns, and orthophoto maps which show elevation contours imposed over an air photo base. There are literally thousands of different types of maps which are created to show an almost unimaginable range of information. For those wishing to learn more about the art of map making, formally known as cartography, there are many excellent books available to read. The resource book used for this primer was *Elements of Cartography* by Robinson, Sale, and Morrison.

Map scale is simply a term which describes the distance and area covered on the map sheet. A "large" scale map describes a small territorial area, while a "small" scale map will cover a much larger area on a similar size sheet. A two by three foot map which shows only downtown

Vancouver is a large scale map. A map of the same size which covers western Canada is a small scale map. For base map purposes, you are thus looking for a small scale map which will cover an area larger than the bioregion you will ultimately be describing. The obvious question then arises: "If I don't know the borders of my bioregion, how can I choose a base map big enough to include it?" There is no easy answer to this question except that you will have to use common sense, and perhaps try out several sizes of base map before settling on one that is appropriate.

There are several general rules of thumb that will help you to initially find bioregions:

- watershed boundaries (major rivers or main tributaries) are the units most often used to define bioregions;
- the watershed(s) in any single bioregion will usually flow to only one ocean (Arctic, Pacific, Atlantic, Gulf of Mexico, etc.);
- bioregions usually relate to biogeoclimatic or ecoregion areas where a particular grouping of vegetation, climate, and landform predominate;
- bioregions often correspond to the territories of single or associated aboriginal peoples;
- your bioregion is likely the region that you know; places that are foreign to you or which are generally unfamiliar are probably "somewhere else;"
- bioregions are rarely defined by state, national, provincial, reservation, or other arbitrary borders.

If this type of approach is too scary, then there are two alternate base map definition options that can be used. Each of these options is time consuming, but may provide the slow introduction to processes that will help build your confidence as a budding reinhabitant cartographer.

The first alternative involves finding out which major watershed you live in and using that area as the initial boundary of your bioregion. The scale of watersheds that should be used for this approach include major tributaries of the Colorado, Mackenzie, Mississippi, Rio Grande, Fraser, Columbia, Peace, Yukon, St. Lawrence, or other similarly large drainage area. Coastal dwellers will want to start with groupings of smaller basins.

Or, if the map library you have found has a large-format copy machine (most do), you can save a lot of time by finding a planimetric map which allows you to copy a relatively large land area on an eleven by seventeen inch sheet. For example, regions appropriate for copying in North America would be the Atlantic drainage, Mississippi drainage, Mackenzie

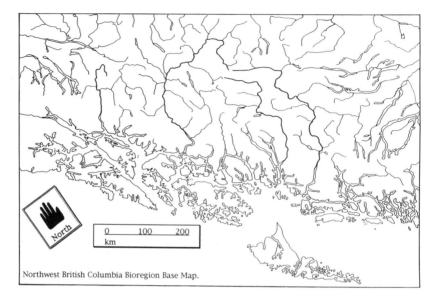

Northwest British Columbia Bioregion Base Map.

drainage, or area west of the continental divide. This image can then be used as a temporary base map on which you can trace a few of the types of bioregion boundaries explained further on in the primer. When the size of your bioregion becomes apparent, you can then make a base map of an appropriate size.

Once you have found an appropriate base map area you should place it on a light table and orient it so that ocean coastlines and/or rivermouths are at the table's bottom edge. This may be a reorientation of the traditional north-south vertical map axis done to reflect the flow of water from the "top" of the bioregion to the "bottom." Simple, uncluttered base maps offer the most flexibility. Next, cover the base map with your tracing paper and lightly follow river, coastline, and island borders only. It is recommended that you leave small circles at the location of settlements, and small crosses to indicate elevations of important peaks. Space should be left at the edges of your tracing paper for a half inch margin and heavy border line that will nicely frame your emerging image of home.

Tracing a base map can be a fascinating experience in bioregion visualization. As your pencil moves along rivers and coastlines, imagine the actual landscapes you are travelling over. If you have chosen the right base map area you should be able to "see" each area of your territory as your pencil moves over the landscape. Remember, the area you are tracing is most likely the region you move through on a regular basis.

Once you have created a base map, make 20 copies on a copy machine. This can be done either at the original eleven by seventeen inch size, or can be reduced to a smaller paper size. As you proceed with the primer exercises, it may be necessary to adapt your base map to cover a larger area. Don't feel bad if you have to do this. The entire bioregion mapping process is an exploration that may take you in directions which are not always predictable.

Example: for Northwest B.C. it was more appropriate to place east at the "top," and west at the "bottom" of the base map image. On the Pacific coast of North America the sun, tides, rivers, salmon and weather travel from east (top) to west (bottom). Several medium size coastal drainage basins were covered, as were the territories of aboriginal nations that share language or trade relationships.

Source: The base map was adapted from a generic map of *Canada* published by the Federal Department of Energy, Mines and Petroleum Resources in 1966.

Each of the next primer exercises should be separately charted on different copies of your own base map.

Historic Political Boundaries

Colonial, territorial, state, provincial and national borders are the lines of legitimacy within which human governance and development are

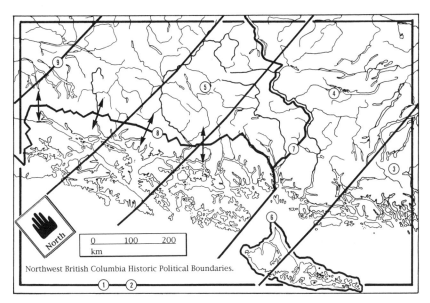

Northwest British Columbia Historic Political Boundaries.

practiced. Over time, these boundaries have changed often to suit the specific needs of political and economic élites that periodically rise and fall from power. It is necessary to visualize how these jurisdictions have evolved for two important reasons. First, it is absolutely essential to understand the political history of your home region. Second, the argument that bioregionalism requires "impossible" changes in spatial governance units falls apart when the historic fickleness of boundary movement is realized.

Example: since 1750, Northwest B.C. has been claimed by five nations who between them established four colonies, three territories, a state, a province, and innumerable municipalities, reserves, and administrative regions. Borders shown correspond to the following boundaries: 1) Spanish territorial claim; 2) Russian territorial claim; 3) New Hanover (Britain); 4) New Cornwall (Britain); 5) New Norfolk (Britain); 6) Queen Charlotte Islands annexed to Vancouver Island Crown Colony (Britain); 7) "Stikeen Territory" (Britain); 8) Russia-Britain, British Columbia-Alaska, U.S.A.-Canada border; 9) Yukon Territory (Canada).

Adapted from sources including: Ireland, William E. "The Evolution Of The Boundaries Of British Columbia," *British Columbia Historical Quarterly* 3.4 (October 1939): 263-282; Van Alstyne, Richard W., "International Rivalries In The Pacific Northwest," *Oregon Historical Quarterly* 46:3 (September 1945): 185-218; Ball, Georgiana, "The Peter Martin Case and the Provisional Settlement of the Stikine Boundary," *B.C. Studies*, 10 (Summer 1971): 35-55; Gibson, James R., *Imperial Russia In Frontier America: The Changing Geography of Supply of Russian America, 1784-1867*, New York: Oxford University Press, 1976.

Source hints: historical journals; provincial, state, national historical atlases; regional histories.

Current Political Division

It is equally important to visualize the major political boundaries which currently dissect your base map area. This image should include national, state/provincial, and possibly county/region limits. The resulting image becomes a representation of the political reality that any bioregionalist must work within. Designing a bioregion utopia is an honorable task, but for such a plan to be implemented some recognition must be given to the structures of governance that must be changed.

In conjunction with your bioregion mapping, it's a good idea to begin reading about the political system that imposes current boundaries across your home area. How have these systems evolved? How are they currently organized, and where is power vested?

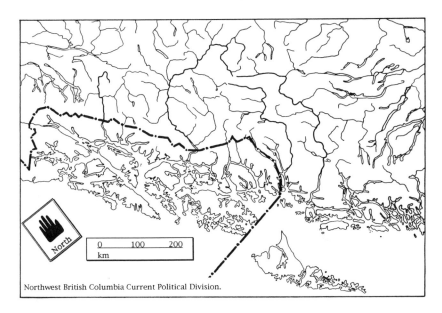

Northwest British Columbia Current Political Division.

Example: the Northwest B.C. base map area is broken by an international division between U.S.A/Canada and Alaska/British Columbia. This division created immense difficulty in gaining mapping information from national and state/province sources which generate information in different locations, formats and levels of detail. Consequently, the bioregion mapping process was heavily concentrated on the Canada/British Columbia portion of the area only. While efforts to rearrange Canadian governance structures is the focus of the primer examples, there has been tentative contact between reinhabitants from Alaska and B.C. which promises rich cooperation.

Source: Fisheries and Environment Canada, Inland Waters Directorate, *British Columbia Active Hydrometric Stations*, map. Ottawa: Inland Waters Directorate, 1978.

Source hints: map library; state, provincial, national atlases; government printing office inquiry; state, or provincial government agency in charge of local government.

Internal Boundaries

The final step towards understanding how your base map area is currently divided involves drawing boundaries used by as many government agencies as can be identified. This exercise will introduce the luckless bioregionalist to the incredible complexity of administrative

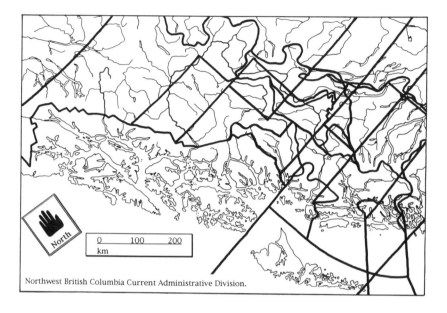

Northwest British Columbia Current Administrative Division.

bureaucracy imposed by central governments. It will also show in a graphic manner how current governance structures exist with little relationship to watershed, landform, or cultural limits. This map, when completed, is a powerful image when describing to others the hodge-podge of boundaries which needlessly place divisions between humans and their supporting natural environments. Administrative units that can be charted include: local governments, natural resource management units (mining, forestry, fisheries, wildlife, agriculture), tax collection districts, electoral areas, census districts, hospital authorities, highways districts, parks, Indian reserves, and area jurisdictions for courts, police, the military, human resources, government agents, etc. Just learning the names and purposes of all these divisions is an experience that will show just how inorganic current governance and development structures have become.

Example: the "internal boundary" map of the Northwest shows the same pattern as a plate of spaghetti randomly splashed on a wall. There is no sense to the confusion of jurisdictions which slice across the land without recognition of human or natural communities. Such boundaries are made for the convenience of centralized governments only, they do not assist residents of Northwest B.C. to conceptualize how a prosperous and self-reliant bioregional culture could be constituted.

Source: British Columbia Ministry of the Environment, *British Colum-*

bia Administrative Areas 1981, map series. Victoria: Surveys and Mapping Branch, 1981.

Source hints: map library; state and provincial atlases; government printing office inquiry; state or provincial government or agency in charge of local government.

Watersheds

Once the human way of making boundaries is understood, it is time to make the same effort learning to identify components of natural systems resident in the base map area. Watershed areas are the most important of these, and can easily be charted by drawing lines around large rivers and their major tributaries. The secret to this exercise is to start by drawing the divide between rivers that flow to different oceans (if any), and then to surround the basins of only the largest watersheds, thus keeping the map area uncluttered with scores of smaller catchments. Major tributaries of larger river systems can then be marked with dashed lines to show how they are internally divided. The joy of marking river boundaries is that they all fit together in a logic of topography. Unlike the slash of most human borders, rivers will begin to show the true shape of your bioregion.

When identifying watershed limits it is useful to think just how pervasive is the force of water. Over the millennia, water in the form of

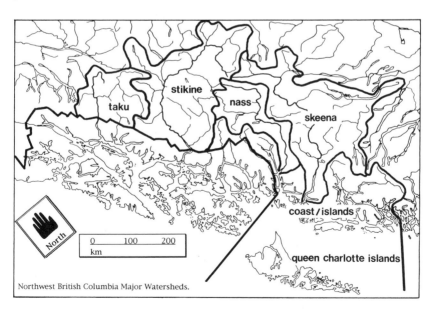

Northwest British Columbia Major Watersheds.

glaciers, oceans and lakes, rivers and streams, tides and currents, rain and snow has etched most of the landscapes on the planet. Equally important, the rate and volume of water cycled through ecosystems is one of the great parameters that define which present interconnections of life can survive in a particular locale. In mapping its flows and limits, water can be appreciated purely for its physical properties. It can also be revered as a transformative element with a power that is as much spiritual as it is material.

Example: Northwest B.C. is drained by four major streams. The large Skeena (21,038 sq. miles), Nass (8,046 sq. miles), Stikine (19,445 sq. miles), and Taku (6,673 sq. miles) rivers all cut through the Coast Ranges and flow to the Pacific. Smaller streams such as the Bear (910 sq. miles), Kitimat (775 sq. miles) and Yakoun (205 sq. miles) drain the Pacific side of the Coast Mountain or parts of hundreds of coastal islands. It is up to the reinhabitant to identify and group these smaller catchments by using his or her knowledge of similarity and proximity. Drainage basins on the edge of the sample base map area flow to the Arctic Ocean, or reach the Pacific far to the south. The mapping of watershed units begins to naturally mark the division between bioregions.

Source: Holland, Stuart S., *Landforms of British Columbia*, British Columbia Department of Mines and Petroleum Resources, Bulletin 48. Victoria: Queen's Printer, 1976. Smaller basin measurements were estimated with the assistance of a planimeter (a device which, when run on the circumference of an irregular area, will provide the area of the territory circumscribed).

Source hint: Wilson, Alfonso, Kathleen T. Iseri, *River Discharge To The Sea From The Shores Of The Conterminous United States, Alaska, and Puerto Rico*, map (2 sheets), Hydrologic Investigations Atlas HA-282. Washington DC: United States Geological Survey, 1969; map library for thematic maps on "hydrology;" national, state, or provincial atlases; state, or provincial environment agency for streamflow monitoring data.

Physiographic Regions

Water, wind, and geologic forces construct landscapes into distinctive shapes and textures. Resulting valleys, plateaus, mountain ranges, lowlands, and plains become the physical stage for all human activity. To chart these areas involves a search for thematic maps which describe physiography: the study of the physical features of the land as defined predominantly by elevation and slope.

Think of the region where you live. Geology, or the subterranean composition of the earth's crust, is exposed at the surface to atmospheric

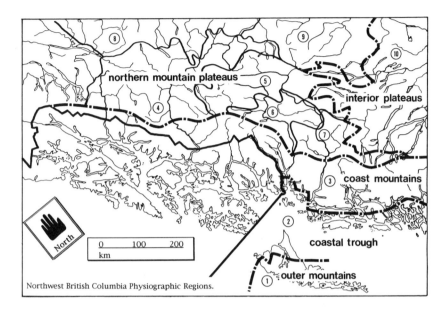

northern mountain plateaus

interior plateaus

coast mountains

coastal trough

North

outer mountains

0   100   200
km

Northwest British Columbia Physiographic Regions.

forces which, over millions of years, have created a highly varied and interlocking puzzle of terrain types. Each landscape has a differing capability to support life, settlements and economic activity. Mountain slopes will be unstable if deforested. Valleys can be rich in water and deep soil, but may flood. A physiographic region tells by its shape and texture just how it can be sustainably stewarded by a resident human population.

Northwest British Columbia Physiographic Regions	
Coastal Systems	*Interior Systems*
1. Insular Mountains	4. Stikine Plateau
2. Hecate Depression	5. Skeena Mountains
3. Coast Mountains	6. Nass Basin
	7. Hazelton Mountains
	8. Cassiar Mountains
	9. Omineca Mountains
	10. Interior Plateau

Example: the northern area of British Columbia appears at a casual glance to be a jumble of indistinguishable mountains. Upon closer view, it is evident that the shape of the land is extremely ordered. The major Northwest B.C. landform division is between Coastal and Interior zones. Within these two areas are ten sub-areas which describe a dominantly mountain area on the Pacific, and a high plateau region inland. Each physiographic region supports different associations of plants and animals—life communities which, when understood, help to further define bioregion borders.

Source: Holland, Stuart S., *Landforms of British Columbia: A Physiographic Outline*, British Columbia Department of Mines and Petroleum Resources, Bulletin 48. Victoria: Queen's Printer, 1976.

Source hints: Fenneman, N.M., "Physiographic divisions of the United States," *Annals of the Association of American Geographers*, 18 (1928): 261-353; state and provincial mining agency maps or publications; university geography texts; national, state, and provincial atlases.

Climate

Yet another natural element that must be considered in bioregion definition is climate. Wind, rain, temperature, snow, length of night and day, intensity of sunlight, and season cycles dictate how life must adapt to any location. For the purposes of this exercise, we are interested only in charting major climate divisions called macroclimates. This would be

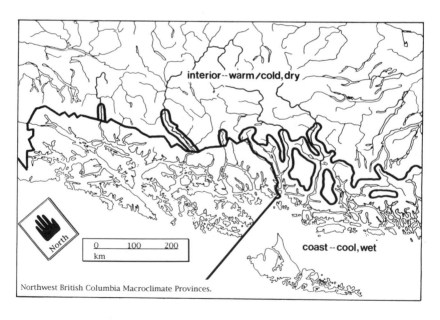

interior--warm/cold, dry

coast--cool, wet

North

0   100   200
km

Northwest British Columbia Macroclimate Provinces.

the division between, say, wet and arid zones, or where temperature regimes change in a discernible manner.

If no pattern emerges from either your regional climatic understanding, or from other available sources, there is another way of defining large areas of similar climate. Köppen used fixed threshold values of temperature and precipitation to classify every area of the Earth into climate zones. Maps showing the distribution of Köppen's classifications are commonly held in map libraries, or are shown in geography texts.

Example: not surprisingly, climate changes in the Northwest follow borders of the two major physiographic zones. The coastal area is cool and very wet, while the interior highlands are dryer, with more defined warm and cold seasons. These divisions correspond to "Cfb" and "Dfc" Köppen classifications. Again, at the edges of the base map area, climates begin to differ either due to changes in latitude, or effects of non-maritime weather patterns.

Sources: Kendrew, W. G., D. Kerr, *The Climate of British Columbia and The Yukon Territory*, Ottawa: Queen's Printer, 1955; Köppen, W., *Grundriss der Klimkunde*, Berlin: Walter de Gruyter, 1931; Regional District of Kitimat-Stikine, *Kitimat-Stikine Regional District Regional Resource Inventory*, map. Terrace, British Columbia: Regional District of Kitimat-Stikine, 1981.

Source hints: national, state, and provincial atlases; state, or provincial environment or agriculture agency for records of climatic norms; university geography library; government printing office inquiry.

Biomes / Biogeoclimatic Zones / Ecoregions

Once the primary physical forces which define landforms are understood, it is necessary to look at how life itself begins to further distinguish bioregion borders. This is a more difficult level of interpretation. It involves the perception of gradients of change between plant and animal communities that can be as sharp as a knife, or feathered into transitions that will only be understood with decades of experience in place. There are a number of techniques that have been devised to represent these areas of common life force, including maps that show how these distribution techniques have been applied over many regions of the planet.

Over the last thirty years, the type and number of classification systems which use combinations of biophysical data to represent "natural" regions of varying definition have multiplied dramatically. A worldwide, multiple-criteria "biogeographical" classification system was pioneered by Dasmann and Udvardy in the early 1970s. A map which resulted from this research was extremely popular, but led to some confusion amongst people who attempted to use it to define their bioregion. The regions shown were powerful indicators of commonality but were massive in size, and without reference to past or present human cultural patterns. In British Columbia, a "biogeoclimatic" classification system was pioneered on a more localized scale by Dr. V. J. Krajina. More recently, "ecoregions" have been delineated for the same area in the work of Dennis Demarchi and others. Each of these techniques, although still without reference to human land occupation parameters, begin to reveal distinct bioregion territories in British Columbia which primarily range in size between approximately 20,000 to 80,000 square miles.

Example: biogeoclimatic or ecoregion mapping was not used as a frame of reference in the original Northwest B.C. mapping study. New developments in the representation of biogeoclimatic zones and ecoregions in the late 1980s, especially in the cartography of Demarchi and Skoda, make the inclusion of this type of information in the future evolution of the primer a delightful necessity.

Sources: Skoda, Louis, *Biogeoclimatic Zones of British Columbia 1988*, map. Victoria: Province of British Columbia. Ministry of Forests, 1988; Demarchi, Dennis, *Ecoregions of British Columbia*, Victoria: British Columbia Ministry of Environment, Wildlife Branch, 1988; Krajina, V. J., R. C. Brooks, eds., *Ecology of Western North America*, vol. 2, nos. 1 and 2, Vancouver: University of British Columbia, Deptartment of Botany, 1970.

Source hints: Omernick, J. M. "Ecoregions of the United States," map. *Annals of the Association of American Geographers*, 77.1: 118-125; U.S. Environmental Protection Agency, *Report of The Ecoregions Subcommittee of The Ecological Processes and Effects Committee: Evaluation of The Ecoregion Concept*, (EPA-SAB-EPEC-91-003), Washington, DC: EPA, January 1991; Bailey, Robert G., Steven C. Zoltai, Ed B. Wiken, "Ecological Regionalization in Canada and the United States," *Geoforum*, 16.3 (1985): 265-275.

Additional Natural Bioregion Border Parameters

Although reliance on summary representations of biophysical personality is a useful shortcut to defining bioregions, it may be that the assessment of individual parameters may be more appropriate in certain locales. The following "ways of seeing" a bioregion are included to give only a hint at the range of ways that unique components of physical territory can be identified and bounded.

Vegetation. Changes in major vegetation types can also be used to define bioregions. Unfortunately for our exercise, there are many ways in which vegetation groupings can be made. Some classification systems are very general, while others are a maze of complexity. To assist in ordering the boundaries of relatively large bioregions, it may be best to use classification techniques which show the distribution of plant communities that existed before the supremacy of industrial agriculture, logging, and mass urbanization. This perception would be a guide to sustainable vegetation association types which would grow without herbicides, pesticides, mass watering, or chemical fertilization.

Example: Northwest B.C. is predominantly covered by ancient forests which, although damaged by industrial logging, still maintain their primal patterns of distribution. Within the northwest bioregion there is again a general division between Coastal Western hemlock and Engleman spruce forest associations which trend along the already established separation between coast and interior.

Source hints: Küchler, A. W., *Potential Natural Vegetation of the Conterminous United States*, map and manual, American Geographical Society Special Publication No. 36. New York: AGS, 1964; Küchler, A. W., Jack McCormick, *Vegetation Maps of North America*, vol. 1 of 5 (world coverage). Lawrence: University of Kansas Libraries, 1965; Küchler, A. W., *Vegetation Mapping*, New York: Ronald Press, 1967; state and provincial agriculture and forestry agencies.

Wildlife. The bioregion mapping process may include description of the territories or habitats of non-rooted species that share your home territory. Because the sheer number of insects, birds, fish and other life forms which inhabit any area is staggering, it will be necessary to limit habitat range mapping to "indicator," or "totem" species that might particularly define non-human life associations. By example, there are relatively strict territories where salmon, buffalo, or polar bears have such a pervasive impact on regions that they may define how they should be bounded. Perhaps the best way to proceed is to choose several "totem" species which, in your perception, are especially indicative of your region, and find out the limits of their pre- and post- industrialized era occupation.

Example: because of its relative isolation, Northwest B.C. is a globally significant refuge for many species of temperate forest wildlife. Due to this abundance, there is no single species whose population range is useful in bounding the bioregion. Totem animals inhabiting the region are salmon, eagles, orca whales and grizzly bears.

Source hints: World Conservation Union, Avenue Mont-Blanc, CH-1196, Gland, Switzerland; state or provincial fish and wildlife agencies; environmental protection organizations; wildlife capability mapping;

environmental impact assessments.

Soils. In areas where the physiography is relatively "flat," it will be especially useful to chart major soil types across a base map area. By understanding soil characteristics you not only begin to gauge crop growing capabilities, but also gain perceptions of subsurface water flow, and the potential of the ground to support construction of settlements and accompanying infrastructure. Soils can be described by their texture, permeability, susceptibility to erosion, profile, or series. It would be prudent to also include consideration of the processes of desertification which may be threatening the ability of soils to support sustainable reinhabitation.

Example: because of recent glaciation, the soils in Northwest B.C. are all less than 12,000 years old and relatively shallow. Soils of any depth tend to collect in narrow river valleys in areas that experience flooding. Charting soil distributions in the mountainous Northwest is not useful in finding bioregion borders.

Source hints: Food and Agriculture Organization of the United States. United Nations Educational, Scientific and Cultural Organization, *Soil Map of the World*, Vol. II: North America. Paris: UNESCO, 1975; United Nations Environment Program, *World Atlas of Desertification*. London: Edward Arnold, 1992; thematic maps on soils; university geology libraries; state or provincial soil surveys; state or provincial agriculture agencies.

Geology / Geomorphology. Rocks that make up the Earth's crust are distinctive by age, origin, and mineral type. The subsurface character of a bioregion will have greatly influenced rates of erosion, how soil is made, the location of aquifers, the stability of slopes, and a host of other environmental factors. Maps can be made to show both the geology of the area (what types of specific rocks are resident), and its geomorphology (how landforms were shaped).

Example: Northwest geology is divided between a coast band of intrusive and metamorphic rocks, and an interior zone of sedimentary and volcanic rocks. The indistinct line where these types of geology meet is at the point where oceanic and continental plates crash together. The slow, violent meeting of these huge masses has caused intricate patterns of melt and fold that host pockets of rich mineralization.

Source hints: thematic maps on geology or geomorphology; university geology libraries; annual reports of provincial or state mining agencies; state or provincial atlases.

Seabed. Many bioregions will border on the sea or other large bodies of water. If there are other bioregions that are adjacent to the same submarine region, then it is important to chart the boundaries which delineate a separation of their stewardship responsibilities. Physical features which mark these separations may be trenches, channels, areas of deep water between islands or other landforms, or may be based on the habitat of certain marine fish or mammal species.

Example: Northwest B.C.'s coast is open to vast stretches of Pacific Ocean and does not require that shared jurisdiction with other bioregions be delineated.

Source hints: Couper, Alistair, ed., *The Times Atlas and Encyclopaedia of the Sea*. London: Times Books, 1989; Food and Agriculture Organization of the United Nations, *Atlas Of The Living Resources Of The Seas*. New York: FAO/Unipub, 1981; marine charts; province or state fishery agencies; international agreements on seabed jurisdiction which are accompanied by maps.

Aboriginal Territories

Settlement areas inhabited and defended by aboriginal peoples are especially relevant to our task of identifying bioregion borders. Because aboriginal nations relied so much on localized sources of natural resources for their survival, they tended to array their activities and settlements in patterns that demonstrated intimate knowledge of carrying capacity. In traditional, pre-industrial era societies resources needed to supply basic human needs were harvested in a yearly "round." Many locations in a territory were used in each season to gain food and material goods. Knowledge of this complex pattern of opportunity was passed on from generation to generation. Reinhabitants can learn important lessons by studying the land use of pre-contact Native cultures resident in their base map area.

Example: sixteen separate tribal groups have inhabited the B.C. Northwest. Their territories cover the entire base map area. These traditional nations are especially important in the Northwest because 20,000 Native people continue to claim sovereignty over their pre-contact holdings. Due to the probable success of "Land Question" disputes currently under negotiation, it is possible that traditional tribal borders will again form the basis of vital governance units. It should be noted that there has yet to be a consensus reached amongst First Nations leaders regarding how many overlapping territorial claims will be resolved.

Source: Duff, Wilson, *The Impact Of The White Man; The Indian History Of British Columbia*, Volume 1, Anthropology In British Columbia, Memoir No. 5. Victoria: Provincial Museum of B.C., 1964.

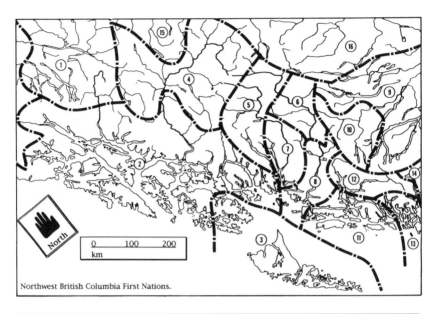

Northwest British Columbia First Nations.

Northwest British Columbia First Nations	
1. Inland Tlingit	9. Carrier
2. Inland Tlingit	10. Wet'suwet'en
3. Haida	11. Southern Tsimshian
4. Tahltan	12. Haisla
5. Tsetsaut	13. Heiltsuk
6. Gitksan	14. Bella Coola
7. Nisga'a	15. Kaska
8. Coast Tsimshian	16. Sekani

Source hints: *Handbook of North American Indians*, in more than ten volumes (by geographic region). Washington DC: Smithsonian Institution, various dates; National Geographic Society, *Indians of North America*, map. No. 02816. Washington DC: NGS, 1982; Price, David H., *Atlas of World Cultures: A Geographical Guide To Ethnographic Literature*. Newbury Park, California: Sage, 1989; First Nation elders; tribal council offices; university anthropology libraries; thematic maps on tribal territories pre- and post-European contact.

Current Use

When defining bioregions it is an absolute necessity to understand how the current human population of any region uses the land. An image should be made showing the location of each settlement. Lines can then be drawn out from each town or city showing where its residents work, play, go to hospital and court, shop, hunt, regularly visit, etc. Without becoming too detailed, this graphic begins to show the spatial relationships which exist both between communities, and between communities and the land. Information required for this primer component is best found by collecting a group of friends and having a discussion around the following topics: Where do people work? Where are natural food sources harvested? Where do we go for recreation? What rural area around each town relies on that town for services? Where do we get medical and other services? This is a fun exercise that continues to illuminate the mix of natural and human elements which will help to map bioregion boundaries.

This exercise would be extremely important if you were trying to ascertain the boundaries of bioregions in areas dominated by large urban settlements. The "footprint" of each city could be discerned through tracing divides that separate commercial center dominance, commuter destination, or even professional sports team allegiance. It would also be useful to draw lines out to sources of energy, water, solid waste refuse sites, and other support services which allow the urban area to exist. Boundaries of "city states" begin to emerge from this type of demarcation — not properly bioregions, but perhaps the spatial area best suited for the transformation of existing urban centers into "ecocities."

Example: there are approximately 50 settlements scattered across the Northwest B.C. base map area, ten of which are home to eighty percent of the current population. By completing the "current use" graphic, it becomes evident that these main settlements are at the center of what can be described as "working circles." It also is evident that the largest settlements such as Terrace and Smithers have "captured" the markets of smaller communities, an indication that the incessant process of centralization is working in the region.

Source hint: gather a group of friends who live in different parts of your area and have them draw the patterns that their regular land use describe.

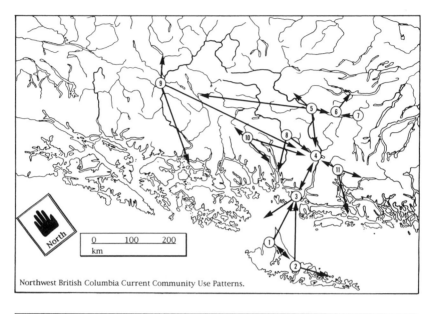

Northwest British Columbia Current Community Use Patterns.

Northwest British Columbia Population Centers.	
1. Masset	7. Houston
2. Queen Charlotte City/Skidegate	8. Aiyansh
3. Prince Rupert	9. Telegraph Creek
4. Terrace	10. Stewart
5. Hazelton	11. Kitimat
6. Smithers	

Special Locations

In every region there are special places which somehow link humans to a spiritual connection with nature. These places are rare, and are usually accepted by residents of a region as locations that will be protected at all costs. Mountains, waterfalls, hot springs, rivers, deep canyons, glaciers, caves, or cherished vistas are the types of portals which lead to mystical or meditative encounter. To map these places on your base map, it is also best to gather a group of reinhabitants and share experiences. It is worthwhile noting that special places tend to be relatively close to an individual's place of residence. Care should be taken to inquire across the base map area to get an equal distribution of sites.

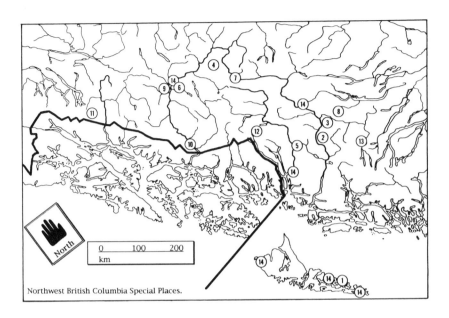

Northwest British Columbia Special Places.

Northwest British Columbia Special Locations	
1. Gwaii Haanas	11. Llewellyn Glacier
2. Seven Sisters Mountains	12. Bear Valley
3. Roche DeBoule Range	13. Nanika Falls
4. Spatsizi Plateau	14. First Nations sites:
5. Nass Lava Beds	—Tahltan-Stikine confluence
6. Ice Mountain	—North Island
7. Triple Divide	—Kisgegas
8. Babine Mountains	—Tanu
9. Eight Mile Creek Waterfall	—Ninstints
10. Great Glacier	

It is in this type of identification that bioregion mapping departs from the kind of land use planning that is commonly imposed by central governments. Bioregion planning would guarantee that areas around sacred sites were protected and linked together in a web of relatively wild land. This pattern would then reveal what remaining areas were available for more intensive human uses. Development would conform to necessities for life and culture, not vice versa.

Example: because it is an isolated wilderness region, Northwest B.C. is home to a great variety of spectacularly beautiful natural features. These sites are known by almost everyone in the region, and are usually visited with reverence and respect. They are also vigorously protected.

Source hint: gather friends!

Soft Boundaries

For the purposes of this primer we have now completed a simple inventory of elements that can help to describe bioregions of a scale which are meaningful to reinhabitants. The next step is to overlay the different base maps, creating a single image representing all the data we have collected. To do this, a base map sheet should be placed over the piled component maps, and a tracing made of the combined image. So that the image is readable, you will have to use a different type of line to represent each of the data types to be traced. If you want to splurge, it would be helpful to invest in fine-line colored felt pens. With creativity and care, it will be possible to "see" your bioregion emerge from the various lines that you will draw.

It is important to understand that bioregions do not always need to have a sharp external boundary. Water catchments may not coincide exactly with climate zones, or aboriginal territories and physiographic regions may not match. These overlaps describe "soft boundaries," or zones that can either be divided by consensus, or may best be administered by the residents of the adjoining bioregions. Remember, there should be two main criteria for the final identification of the borders of a "life place" region. First, the area chosen should be strongly linked to continuities of resident physical or ecological elements. Second, the bioregion should represent the common sphere of activity shared by a group of traditional and/or present communities. A fairly compartmentalized territory will usually emerge from this assessment.

Example: borders of the Northwest B.C. bioregion define themselves. Watersheds are the dominant natural element, and are closely matched by physiographic and climate zones. Aboriginal and Euro-Canadian settlement and current use patterns also closely match watershed boundaries. In addition, there is an obvious internal division between a coastal and interior climate, culture, and physiography. Even though newly mapped, the Northwest bioregion is obviously a territory that has existed for thousands of years. It is an area that is ecologically whole. It is also an area that has supported an interrelated, if bioregionally unconscious, group of humans within its borders since before the beginning of time.

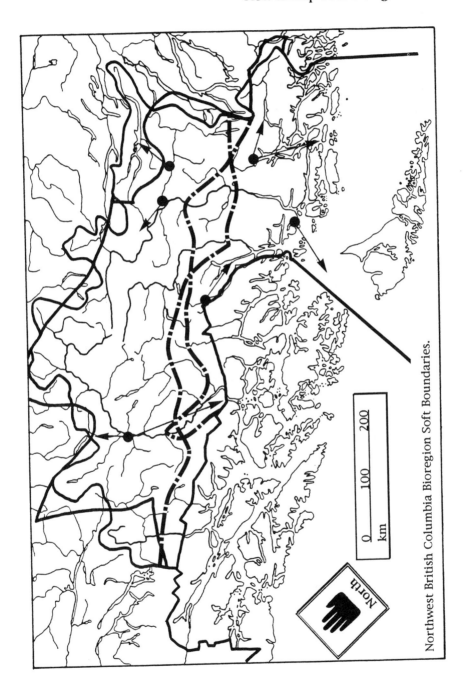

Northwest British Columbia Bioregion Soft Boundaries.

Bioregion Boundaries

It is now time to take the soft boundary scribbling just finished and recopy the image in a more formal manner. With a final base map sheet, trace a single line that, to the best of your understanding, represents your bioregion. This final graphic should then be put away for a few days, or passed around to friends and colleagues. Over time, the borders of your new bioregion should be reconsidered, changed, or simply left to solidify as a powerful life-guiding perception. To a reinhabitant, bioregion borders are far more potent than effete markings chosen by distant politicians. Your territory becomes more than a flag, or a memorized state or provincial capital, or a rare chance to cast a ballot.

The identification of bioregions will allow a reorientation of human allegiance away from nation states and consumerism. Sustainably configured societies would grow in symbiosis with the natural capabilities of land and water environments to sustain use. While confederal associations of bioregions may maintain names like Canada, the United States, or Mexico, the focus of human ingenuity would be radically shifted to the evolution of regionalized cultures. Bounded only by the imperatives for social justice and the conservation of life within ecological carrying capacities, a healthy spectrum of social identities would develop. And the new measure of economic success would be the degree to which all bioregions could be assisted in achieving prosperous self-reliance and a high quality of life.

Example: the Northwest British Columbia Bioregion covers 64,000 square miles of mainland, 40,000 square miles of Pacific Ocean, and 1325 islands totalling another 6,000 square miles. It is a home region to 80,000 people who share complex interrelationships with each other and the land.

The next section of the mapping primer introduces the type of knowledge that will be required if bioregionalists are to evolve sustainable institutions in their newly described territories.

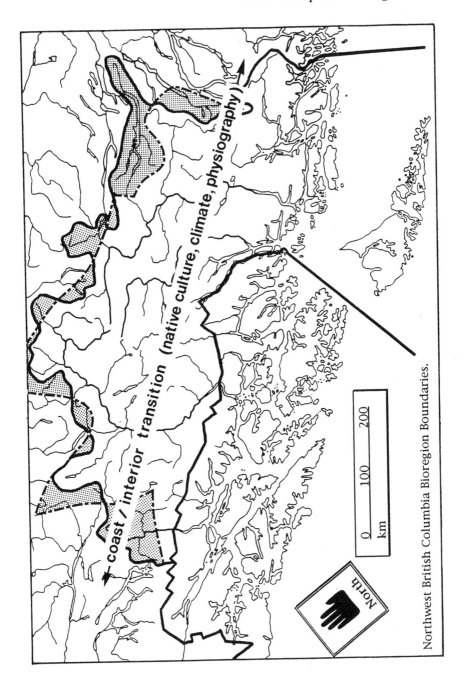

coast / interior transition (native culture, climate, physiography)

Northwest British Columbia Bioregion Boundaries.

0   100   200
km

North

◆

Section 2:
Internal Bioregion Boundaries

Once the task of identifying external bioregion borders is complete, it is necessary to learn about the territory enclosed by the new boundaries. This is a much more demanding exercise. To live within the ability of habitats to support life without significant deterioration, within "carrying capacity," requires a high degree of functional knowledge. To "feel" that your home area can support an environmentally-sound culture and economy is fine, but the responsibility now exists to actually build a working bioregional alternative within fairly exacting limits.

A bioregion is a living organism. Land, water, animals, climate, and other elements in nature interact in a complex web of connectedness. Those who have developed industrial technology ignore working with natural systems, favoring a pillage mentality that ultimately destroys rather than nurtures. This approach to land use is simple, requiring only a knowledge of machines and mining economics, and a blind trust that technology will "fix" all social and environmental ills. A bioregional culture that lives as part of a landscape will need to understand appropriate scale machine technology *and* how forces of land and life weave patterns of sustainable opportunity. For the most part, this information will not be conveniently found in existing books, by categorical listing in government reports, or as part of any academic curricula.

The basic research skills that were learned in Section 1 will help you to find the detailed data necessary to complete the following exercises. Each of these tasks involves pulling facts from many sources and compiling them in a new way. This means learning the boundaries of reporting areas, understanding how units of measure have evolved, and where some obscure report is hidden that unlocks a technique that relates past to present, use to benefit, or profit to impact. This task is more time consuming than difficult, but will require a persistent sleuthing into many libraries and archives. When your investigations are complete, however, your reward will be a description of "home" that has, in all probability, never before existed. More important, through completion of this process you will have been be invested with great power — a perception of the true identity and potential of place.

Photocopy 20 copies of your final bioregion boundary base map. Trace each of the following exercises on an individual boundary map sheet.

Bioregion Climate Station Locations

Many requirements for human survival directly depend upon adaptation to bioregion climate. Food production, water availability, shelter type, and energy needs all are regulated by the various flows of solar energy which define hot and cold, wet and dry, light and dark. To understand these flows requires that you achieve a comprehensive understanding of bioregion climate characteristics at the local level. The first step towards reaching this goal is to compile a list of all climate reporting stations that have been historically located in your bioregion. Records of these stations are kept by national, provincial, or state weather and agricultural agencies. The location of each station should be charted on the base map, and represented by a number which can then be used as a key to additional layers of information explained next in the primer.

It is important to emphasize that the collection and display of climatic information should not be regarded as an end in itself. Functional knowledge of many microclimates must be gained if food is to be grown within the carrying capacity of localized environments. Practical exploration of the potential of bioregions to support sustainable food production, and other human activities, is explained by the "new" discipline of permaculture. As defined by the originator of the concept, Bill Mollison:

> Permaculture (permanent agriculture) is the conscious design and maintenance of agriculturally productive ecosystems which have the diversity, stability, and resilience of natural ecosystems. It is the harmonious integration of landscape and people providing their food, energy, shelter, and other material and non-material needs in a sustainable way. Without permanent agriculture there is no possibility of a stable social order.

> The philosophy behind permaculture is one of working with, rather than against, nature; protracted and thoughtful observation rather than protracted and thoughtless action; of looking at systems in all their functions, rather than only asking one yield of them; and of allowing systems to demonstrate their own evolutions. (Mollison:1992, ix-x)

Example: even though Northwest B.C. is an isolated region with a low

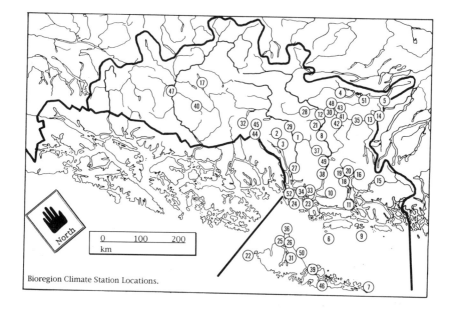

Bioregion Climate Station Locations.

human population, 52 climate stations have been identified. Some of these locations operated for only a short period of time, but are nonetheless useful in exposing the potential of highly localized microclimates to support sustainable human populations.

Source: Environment Canada, *Canadian Climate Normals*, 7 volumes. Ottawa: Queen's Printer, 1982.

Source hints: Mollison, William, *Permaculture: A Practical Guide for a Sustainable Future*, Washington DC: Island Press, 1990; The *Permaculture Activist: A Quarterly Voice for Permaculture in North America*, subscription information available from Route 1, Box 38, Primm Springs, TN 38476, U.S.A.; climate statistics compiled at the state, provincial, and national levels, typically by weather-related or agriculture agencies.

Bioregion Climate Station Location Key

Once climate stations have been identified, a table can be made that lists their exact location. This table should include station name, latitude, longitude, resident river basin, and elevation above or below sea level. By both mapping and listing bioregion climate stations, it is possible to easily show other reinhabitants the spatial distribution of the climate data you have collected.

The strategy behind your collection of bioregional data now begins to become clearer. Climate is not just a weather report on the television.

Bioregion Climate Station Location Key.

No./Place	Location Latitude	Longitude	River Basin	Dist. From Pacific (KM)[1]	Elevation Above Sea (M)
1. Aiyansh	55 12	129 03	Nass	80	152
2. Alice Arm 1	55 28	129 30	Kitsault	5	314
3. Alice Arm 2	55 28	129 28	Kitsault	0	2
4. Fort Babine	55 19	126 37	Skeena	305	719
5. Babine Lk. (Pinkut Ck.)	54 27	125 27	Skeena	402	713
6. Bonilla Is.	53 30	130 38	Bonilla Is.	0	16
7. Cape St. James	51 56	131 01	Kunghit Is.	0	89
8. Cedarvale	55 02	128 18	Skeena	190	152
9. Ethelda B.	53 03	126 33	Estevan Is.	0	8
10. Falls River	53 58	129 45	Falls	60	5
11. Hartley Bay	53 25	129 15	Douglas Chan.	0	12
12. Hazelton	55 12	127 44	Skeena	250	122
13. Houston	54 23	126 43	Bulkley	275	587
14. Houston (CDA)	54 23	126 40	Bulkley	275	585
15. Kemano	53 34	127 56	Kemano	0	70
16. Kildala	53 50	128 29	Kildala	0	30
17. Kinaskan Lk.	57 32	130 12	Iskut	235	315
18. Kitimat	54 00	128 42	Kitimat	0	17
19. Kitimat (T)	54 03	128 38	Kitimat	0	128
20. Kitimat (2)	54 00	128 42	Kitimat	0	2
21. Kitwanga	55 07	128 03	Skeena	210	193
22. Langara Is.	54 15	133 03	Langara Is.	0	41
23. Lawyer Is.	54 07	130 20	Lawyer Is.	0	5
24. Lucy Is.	54 18	130 37	Lucy Is.	0	5
25. Masset	54 02	132 08	Graham Is.	0	3
26. Masset (CFB)	54 02	132 04	Graham Is.	0	12
27. Mill Bay	55 00	129 45	Nass	0	3
28. Murder Ck.	55 31	127 48	Kispiox	275	244
29. Nass Camp	55 18	129 01	Nass	120	152
30. New Hazelton	55 14	127 36	Skeena	250	314
31. Port Clements	53 41	132 11	Graham Is.	0	8
32. Premier	56 03	130 01	Salmon	24	418
33. Prince Rupert	54 17	130 23	Kaien Is.	0	52
34. Prince Rupert (A)	54 18	130 26	Kaien Is.	0	34
35. Quick	54 24	126 55	Bulkley	250	700
36. Rose Spit	54 10	131 40	Graham Is.	0	2
37. Rosswood	54 51	128 48	Kitsumkalum	160	183
38. Salvus Camp	54 18	129 22	Skeena	70	15
39. Sandspit A	53 15	131 49	Moresby Is.	0	5
40. Shaft Ck.	57 21	131 00	Mess	180	914
41. Smithers A	54 49	127 11	Bulkley	290	523
42. Smithers CDA	54 44	127 06	Bulkley	290	515
43. Smithers 4E	54 47	127 05	Bulkley	290	578
44. Stewart	55 57	129 59	Bear	0	12
45. Stewart A	55 57	129 59	Bear	0	5
46. Tasu	52 46	132 03	Moresby Is.	0	15
47. Telegraph Ck.	57 54	131 10	Stikine	210	183
48. Telkwa	54 39	126 50	Bulkley	230	683
49. Terrace A	54 28	128 35	Skeena	120	217
50. Tlell	53 29	131 56	Graham Is.	0	5
51. Topley Lnd.	54 49	126 10	Bulkley	340	722
52. Triple Is.	54 18	130 51	0	0	3

[1]distance from salt water via shortest Valley route distances are approximate.

Source: Comp. from Canada. Env. Canada (1982).

A detailed understanding of climate profiles in scores of local areas indicates what kind and volume of food can be grown, how sturdily buildings must be constructed, and what technologies might be used to provide human comfort and sustainable prosperity. This is the functional level of information that reinhabitants seek — facts that have the ability to empower transformative change.

Example: a listing of climate stations begins to show in even greater detail the surprising number of places that have been inhabited in British Columbia's Northwest. An addition to the list completed for the Northwest is a figure showing climate station distance from the Pacific Ocean by the nearest valley route. Because Northwest weather is mostly dictated by the degree of maritime influence, this data begins to communicate how a more dispersed and self-reliant bioregion settlement pattern might be shaped.

Source: Environment Canada, *Canadian Climate Normals*, 7 volumes. Ottawa: Queen's Printer, 1982.

Source hints: climate statistics compiled at the state, provincial, and national levels, typically by weather-related or agriculture agencies.

Bioregion Microclimate Profiles

With the location of climate stations established, it is now possible to recombine individual station data into functional profiles. This table should be set up in eleven columns as follows:
- Climate station number from base map
- Climate station name
- Total mean rainfall
- Total mean snowfall
- Total precipitation
- Days of measurable rain
- Days of measurable snow
- Greatest precipitation in 24 hours
- Mean daily temperature
- Extreme maximum temperature
- Extreme minimum temperature

This table can be adapted to include any range of microclimate information available in your home bioregion. A further step would be to visit the reporting station sites to take soil samples, photographs of native species, and impressions of resources available for stewardship.

Example: climate profiles were compiled for 26 of the 52 reporting stations in Northwest B.C. This representative sample shows the tremendous climatic diversity between locations throughout the bioregion.

Bioregion Microclimate Profiles.

Place	Total Mean Rainfall mm	Total Mean Snowfall cm	Total Precipitation mm	Days of Meas. Rain	Days of Meas. Snow	Greatest Precip. 24 Hrs. mm	Mean Daily Temp. C°	Extr. Max. Temp. C°	Extr. Min. Temp. C°
1 Aiyansh	807.9	379.0	1136.0	133	55	94.0	-	-	-
2 Alice Arm 1	1336.0	840.8	2073.8	150	85	148.3	4.5	33.9	-25.0
4 Fort Babine	339.8	260.6	600.5	68	52	77.5	1.2	32.8	-44.4
5 Babine Lake	-	265.2	-	-	53	42.8	-	33.9	-44.4
6 Bonilla Is.	2041.0	62.5	2103.6	213	14	87.6	8.0	23.4	-15.0
7 Cape St. James	1481.1	51.3	1531.6	231	23	63.5	8.4	28.3	-12.2
9 Ethelda Bay	3040.2	143.9	3186.0	226	27	129.8	7.7	29.4	-16.7
10 Falls River	3358.7	346.8	3705.8	201	37	183.4	-	-	-
12 Hazelton	430.0	172.8	624.6	117	52	42.9	4.3	36.7	-36.0
15 Kemano	1584.7	296.0	1867.0	158	42	126.2	6.5	37.8	-24.4
16 Kildala	1793.6	331.4	2179.9	190	36	122.4	6.3	33.9	-23.9
19 Kitimat (T)	1753.0	548.3	2298.9	165	47	144.8	6.4	36.1	-25.0
21 Kitwanga	441.6	170.1	616.0	103	42	49.4	4.8	37.2	-35.5
25 Masset	1353.0	87.7	1433.9	200	16	76.2	7.6	28.9	-18.9
30 New Hazelton	395.0	141.6	535.3	87	31	55.9	4.4	36.1	-45.0
31 Port Clements	1437.3	87.5	1535.3	200	13	53.8	7.5	30.0	-17.2
33 Prince Rupert	2334.9	84.1	2403.1	223	18	141.0	7.4	32.3	-21.1
35 Quick	305.8	164.3	488.5	91	56	46.7	-	-	-
37 Rosswood	814.9	243.9	1072.1	149	41	116.1	5.5	36.1	-32.2
39 Sandspit A	1199.7	85.4	1281.0	201	20	79.5	7.9	27.8	-13.9
41 Smithers A	331.2	221.6	522.2	97	75	61.0	3.5	34.4	-43.9
44 Stewart	1304.9	556.0	1894.8	114	52	177.8	5.2	34.4	-30.0
46 Tasu	4172.7	75.7	4217.9	220	15	194.0	8.2	33.3	-11.1
47 Telegraph Ck.	227.1	137.6	376.6	77	48	39.6	2.0	36.0	-41.7
48 Telkwa	283.4	203.8	468.3	86	61	61.7	2.9	37.8	-41.1
49 Terrace A	934.3	403.0	1313.2	150	65	114.8	5.9	35.6	-26.7

Source: Comp. from Canada. Env. Canada (1982).

The word "raincoast" is commonly used to describe the area around Prince Rupert. This word takes on new meaning when it is revealed that Prince Rupert averages 241 days of measurable rain or snow a year. Fort Babine is much drier, but is both colder and has more snow. The creation of climate profiles is useful in translating talk of weather patterns into a more potent force of self-reliant adaptation.

Source: Environment Canada, *Canadian Climate Normals*, 7 volumes. Ottawa: Queen's Printer, 1982.

Source hints: climate statistics compiled at the state, provincial, and national levels, typically by weather-related or agriculture agencies.

Bioregion Growing Seasons

To grow food in a manner that respects the capability of local environments to supply plant and animal energy for human consumption on a sustainable basis requires great understanding of climate cycle and variation. The following information is needed to assess the most basic potential of any specific location to support permaculture:

- Climate station number from base map
- Climate station name
- Average on record — frost free period
- Average on record — last Spring frost
- Average on record — first Fall frost
- Full record extreme — earliest last Spring frost
- Full record extreme — latest last Spring frost
- Full record extreme — earliest first Fall frost
- Full record extreme — latest first Fall frost
- Full record extreme — longest frost free period (dates and days)
- Full record extreme — shortest frost free period (dates and days).

Appropriate technology can be used to extend the ability of local environments to provide food. Greenhouses can be constructed to start seedlings, or to grow species of plants that need more heat or protection than the open air allows. Heat exhausted from hot springs, energy production, or manufacturing processes can be utilised for greenhouse use. Reinhabitation is not a jail sentence to a primitive existence; it a commitment to a complexity that delivers maximum prosperity from minimal disruption of natural systems.

Example: growing season statistics were available for only 39 Northwest B.C. climate stations. Frost-free period averages vary from a respectable 272 days on a coastal island, to a meagre 57 days at an inland aboriginal community. Most surprising was the fact that stations located very close together had such differing frost-free records. This may be that

Bioregion Solar Income.

No./Place	Year Ave. (K.P.H.)	Wind Max Gust. (K.P.H.)	Max. Hr. Speed (K.P.H.)	Degree Days Above 0°C	Degree Days Below 0°C	Average Yearly Bright Sun (Hrs.)
2. Alice Arm 1				2131.0	493.2	
4. Ft. Babine				2052.6		
5. Bonilla Is.				1765.6	1311.5	
6. Bonilla Is.	28.7		143	2982.9	46.4	
7. Cape St. James	33.7	193	177	3102.7	17.5	
9. Ethelda Bay	12.2		60	2885.5	60.8	
12. Hazelton				2461.1	864.5	
15. Kemanto				2681.9	325.2	
16. Kildala				2597.9	301.1	
19. Kitimat T.	12.2		56	2712.0	362.9	1400
20. Kitimat 2						1071
21. Kitwanga				2506.6	762.4	
23. Lawyer Is.	16.8		84			
24. Lucy Is.	20.9		105			
25. Masset				2846.4	65.4	
30. New Hazel on				2400.8	798.7	
31. Port Cle ents				2805.7	88.9	
33. Prince Rupert						985
34. Prince Rupert A	14.8	137	93	2806.2	87.6	1224
36. Rose Spit	26.6		97			
37. Rosswood				2571.1	541.8	
39. Sandspit A	17.6	164	129	2953.6	43.6	1496
41. Smithers A	7.3	114	66	2212.4	934.7	1693
42. Smithers CDA						1602
45. Stewart A				2320.3	418.6	949
46. Tasu				3039.0	32.2	
47. Telegraph Ck.				2263.8	1512.7	
48. Telkwa				2077.2	996.2	
49. Terrace A	14.4	121	89	2615.7	456.4	1405
51. Topley Lnd.						1682
52. Triple Is.	27.0		103			

Source: Comp. from Canada. Env. Canada (1982).

data was kept for only a short, unrepresentative period, but can also be an indication of the radical differences in microclimate that can be effected by small differences in exposure to sunlight, altitude, open water, or floral cover.

Source: Environment Canada, *Canadian Climate Normals*, 7 volumes. Ottawa: Queen's Printer, 1982.

Source hints: climate statistics compiled at the state, provincial, and national levels, typically by weather-related or agriculture agencies.

Bioregion Solar Income

All energy which exists on Earth originates with the sun. Industrial culture has relied on non-renewable, or "fixed," energy sources which include coal, oil, and nuclear fuels to propel development. Reinhabitant cultures would look more towards renewable energy sources, or those fuels which continuously flow through ecosystems in the form of sunlight, wind, water, or biomass. It is not a coincidence that information on these types of "solar income" is very hard to find. With a bit of effort

it should be possible to locate sketchy data for a solar income table with the following data categories:
- Climate station number
- Climate station name
- Wind — yearly average speed
- Wind — maximum recorded gust
- Wind — maximum hourly speed
- Solar — degree days above 0 degrees C or F
- Solar — degree days below 0 degrees C or F
- Solar — average bright sunshine hours.

Example: solar income data was found for only 31 Northwest B.C. climate stations. Again, great differences between areas within the bioregion were evident. Maximum wind gusts as high as 193 kilometres per hour have been recorded, a speed that would destroy many existing wind generators. Degree day totals above zero degrees are roughly equal for coast and inland locations, but time below zero degrees is markedly higher inland. This characteristic is due to the fact that temperatures are relatively steady on the coast, and more extreme inland. Bright sunshine hours are highest inland by a margin of nearly 60 percent. Solar income information begins to show the bioregionalist where certain agricultural activities are best undertaken, what tolerances heating and cooling systems should operate within, and what energy may be available from sun or wind sources.

Source: Environment Canada, *Canadian Climate Normals*, 7 volumes. Ottawa: Queen's Printer, 1982.

Source hints: climate statistics compiled at the state, provincial, and national levels, typically by weather-related or agriculture agencies.

Bioregion River Discharge Cycles

Because watershed areas play such an important role in bioregion identification, an effort should be made to better understand the "personality" of rivers which occupy different catchments. Each river has changing rates of flow that are calculated at various gauging stations. This data is collected for a variety of purposes, but predominantly for flood control prediction.

Historically, many settlements have been built on margins of rivers, seas, or riparian zones. This settlement pattern requires construction of expensive and dubiously effective flood control structures which can damage natural systems. A bioregional approach to this problem would be to learn the patterns of water flow and surge, and to minimize permanent uses in these zones.

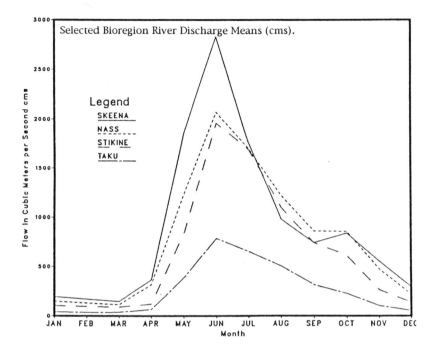

Selected Bioregion River Discharge Means (cms).

To make an image showing discharge patterns for streams in your bioregion, a new skill must be mastered. Flow rates are reported in monthly amounts — figures that are easily graphed to show yearly trends. Graph paper with one quarter inch squares can be purchased for this use. First, mark off horizontal columns two squares wide for each month of the year. This is your "x" axis which measures time. The height of these columns will depend on the highest rate of flow in your discharge data. If you have 30 squares to work with, and the highest reported flow is 3,000 cubic meters per second (cms), then each vertical unit would be worth 100 cms. This is the "y" axis which measures rate of flow. Finally, you can mark in each month's column the flow reported in your data with either "bars," or points that can later be connected.

Example: discharge data was graphed for the four largest Northwest B.C. bioregion rivers. Recorded flow rates varied between almost zero cubic meters per second to a high of nearly 3,000 cubic meters per second. Flow trends for all the streams were remarkably similar, peaking in early June, receding to a lower peak in October when early snows typically melt, and lowering further over winter.

Source: Environment Canada, Inland Waters Directorate, Water Resources Branch, Water Survey of Canada, *Historical Streamflow Summary:*

British Columbia. Ottawa: Ministry of Supply and Services, 1982.
    Source hint: environment agencies; flood control agencies; thematic maps on the topic of hydrology.

Bioregion Population

Just as water flows can be graphed, so can fluctuations in human population levels be identified. The knowledge of how humans have multiplied or declined in a bioregion will help a reinhabitant in several ways. Eras in bioregion history can be indicated. Cycles in economic activity which rise and fall based on resource availability, or condition of export markets, will be revealed. Figures may indicate movement towards metropolitan centralization, or changes in population distribution by age, sex, or income. Analysis of demographic trends may provide an initial indication of the level of population your bioregion can support on a sustainable basis.

Due to the general availability of census data, and the small size of "enumeration" areas that this information is collected within, detailed demographic profiles for a bioregion can be created relatively easily. Once this data base is accessed, there are an almost endless variety of ways that population and related characteristics of human populations

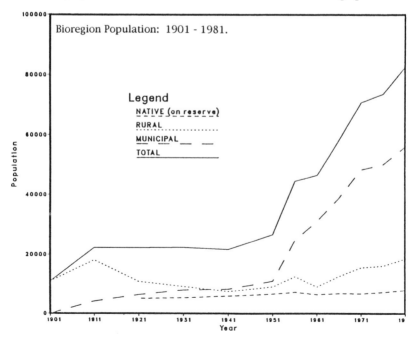

Bioregion Population: 1901 - 1981.

Legend
NATIVE (on reserve)
RURAL
MUNICIPAL
TOTAL

can be compiled. Summaries of census information are widely available, as are computer data bases which allow users to combine information in any form they wish.

The bioregional alternative is as much concerned with achieving social justice as it is with stewarding life within ecological carrying capacities. This means that issues such as the elimination of poverty, gender equality, equal opportunity for minorities, and participation of the mentally or physically challenged in community life will have extremely high priority. The study of census information may be a first step in better understanding these and other social justice issues that will require urgent action.

Example: Northwest B.C. supported a population of approximately 30,000 Native people prior to contact with Europeans. After contact, disease wiped out two-thirds of these original inhabitants. The bioregion's population remained fairly steady at 20,000 until after World War II, when large resource extraction companies were given control of forest, mineral, and energy resources. Since 1950, the number of humans residing in Northwest B.C. has quadrupled to 80,000. From the mid-1970s onward, employment opportunities for aboriginal people, women, and local residents have decreased as technological change reduced the need for wage inputs. Although the source of great wealth for central governments, northern British Columbia continues to be serviced with roads, hospital services, and cultural amenities to a lesser degree than are southern regions.

Source: Canada, *Census of Canada (1901, 1911, 1921, 1951, 1971, 1981)*.

Source hints: museum and archive records; national census records; demographic, planning, and economic development studies carried out by various levels of government.

Bioregion Human Settlement Patterns

The way in which bioregion inhabitants have historically distributed their settlements is a clear indication of how they interact with the land. In most bioregions of North America there have been three eras of settlement that show how bioregion land use trends have evolved. First, the way aboriginal people lived on the land should be represented on the bioregion base map. Draw a small circle for every aboriginal land use site that you can find documented. If the data exists, it would also be beneficial to use different symbols to identify permanent villages, trading sites, shamanic sites, fishing and hunting sites, etc. Second, choose a time when non-Indians first settled your bioregion and mark this occupation pattern on another base map. Use a small circle for

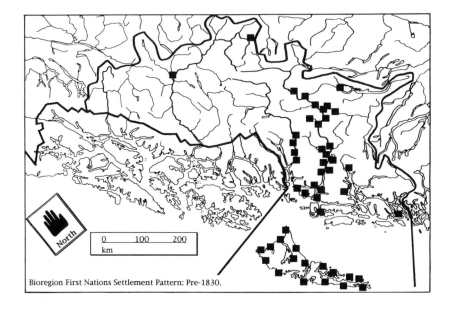

Bioregion First Nations Settlement Pattern: Pre-1830.

communities under 500, a small triangle for towns up to 5,000, and a larger square for any cities that had a larger population. Third, look at the current distribution of population in your bioregion and use the same value symbols to chart urban areas on another base map.

Example: In northwest B.C., the historic Native settlement pattern shows an intricate understanding of the productive capabilities of the bioregion. Villages were typically small and located in protected locations close to major barriers to salmon migration. A large number of widely distributed sites were used to exploit dozens of seasonally available sources of food and material goods. Hunting camps were spaced in such a manner as to crop different animal species at intervals which guaranteed a sustainable harvest.

Non-Native pioneers who settled the bioregion were concentrated into small settlements, but nonetheless were still intimately tied to the land. The use of intermediate technology to harvest and process natural resources allowed an affluence that for many decades nurtured a rich bioregion culture and economy. Scores of sites that had varying capability to support small sawmills, mines, canneries, agriculture, or the efficient distribution of goods and services became natural and logical locations for settlements.

The current bioregion settlement pattern graphically shows the impact of imposed centralization. Several large communities are now home

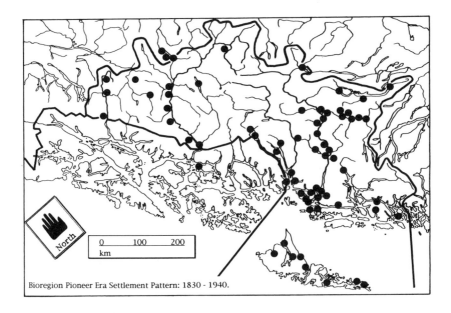

Bioregion Pioneer Era Settlement Pattern: 1830 - 1940.

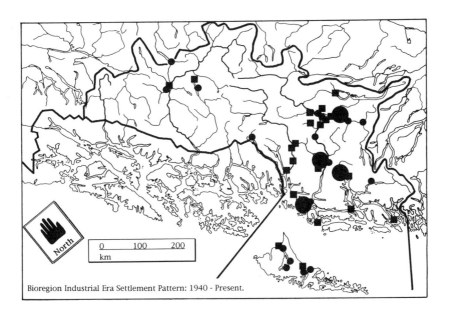

Bioregion Industrial Era Settlement Pattern: 1940 - Present.

to the great majority of bioregion residents. Productive sites that are no longer convenient to chain-store marketing, or large-scale conversion of natural resources for export, lie either abandoned or underdeveloped. Government services are concentrated in the same pattern as that of industrial capital, with the trend continuing towards the support of fewer services in fewer settlements.

Source: compiled from Allaire, Louis, "A Native Mental Map of Coast Tsimshian Villages," *The Tsimshian: Images of the Past; Views for the Present,* Ed. Margaret Seguin. Vancouver: UBC Press, 1984. 82-98; Dalzell, Kathleen, *The Queen Charlotte Islands: 1774-1966.* Terrace, B.C.: C.M. Adam, 1968; Duff, Wilson, *The Impact of the White Man. The Indian History Of British Columbia,* Vol. 1, Anthropology in British Columbia, Memoir No. 5. Victoria: Provincial Museum of B.C., 1964; Regional District of Kitimat-Stikine, *Regional Resource Inventory,* map. Terrace, B.C.: Kitimat-Stikine Regional District, 1981.

Source hint: census data; local history books; old maps and atlases.

◆

Section 3:
Bioregion Economic Structure

We have now described both the external boundaries, and some internal characteristics, of our bioregions. The next task is to study the past economy of these territories in order to gain additional levels of perception. By learning at what rates natural resources have been harvested, we can begin to see the impact humans have had through logging, fishing, agriculture, and mining. This information, in the form of one hundred year or more harvest trends at the species and mineral type level, will also indicate the past and present "wealth" of any bioregion. Harvest volumes, translated into monetary value, will begin to reveal what type of economy a semi-autonomous bioregion could support.

By comparing harvest values with amounts reinvested by governments and corporations, reinhabitants will also be able to judge the benevolence or malevolence of those who currently control the bioregion from outside. Data of this type is very hard to come by. If you are lucky, and your bioregion conforms to government agency administrative units, various kinds of extraction data will be found as a single figure in government reports. If you are unlucky, your task will be to compile this information from scratch, literally having to build a bioregion economic history from scattered sources and assumptions.

The result of this type of inquiry will aid in the conceptualization of how a bioregion economy can be grown. The diagram that follows represents only the simplest of models, but it hints at the way natural capital would be extracted on a sustainable basis, and primarily used for self-reliance production within the bioregion, with prudent exports made to enable goods not available in the bioregion to be imported.

Although this is the most difficult part of the bioregion mapping process, it can also be the most rewarding. As you begin to understand the wealth of your home territory, it is an easy step to visualize what a bioregional alternative for your home region might look like. To demonstrate this vision as it might apply to the Northwest, each of the following assessments concludes with a short paragraph that provides only a hint of promise that a bioregional stewardship regime could offer.

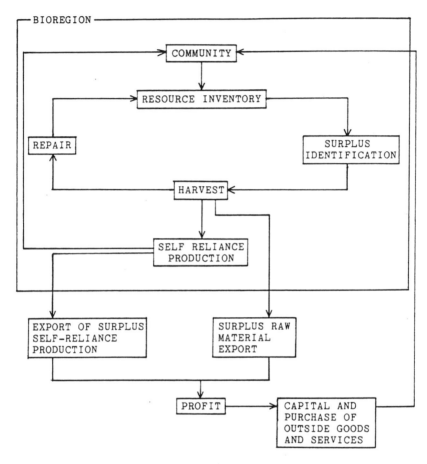

Proposed Bioregion Economic Model.

Bioregion Fishing Industry Profile

If you live in a bioregion where a commercial fishery exists, it will be possible to graph extraction levels of the various species which have been exploited. Catch records have been kept for upwards of two hundred years in many regions of North America. Harvests by species and weight are generally recorded by either port of receipt or, in more recent times, by area of catch. It should be relatively easy to match catch zones to the bioregion borders you have delineated.

It is important to choose a unit of measure which allows simple visualization of the harvest volumes involved. In some cases it will be appropriate to use weight. A more "bioregional" approach may be to graph the numbers of fish harvested, thus reinforcing the perception that each figure on your graph represents what were once living beings.

Catch data should be plotted in graph form. Each year of harvest should be marked on the "x" axis, and the yearly harvest amount will fill the column to the appropriate level on the "y" axis.

Example: the Northwest Bioregion's oldest surviving large-scale industry is based on fishing for herring, halibut, and six species of salmonids. Although many other species are caught in quantity for export, none approaches the value or volume of these major target populations. To communicate a bioregional perspective of fisheries exploitation, a map of catch areas was made, and 14 extraction trend graphs created for the period 1877- 1982 (two only are provided for illustration):

- Bioregion annual herring catch by landed weight;
- Bioregion annual halibut catch by landed weight;
- Bioregion annual salmonid catch by numbers of Pinks, Sockeye, Chinook, Chum, Coho, and Steelhead;
- Bioregion annual salmonid catch by species, weight and numbers;
- Annual salmonid catch by numbers for Skeena, Nass, Queen Charlotte Islands, and Butedale-Gardner catch regions;
- Annual cases of salmonids packed by Nass and Skeena River canneries 1877-1958.

Example: what do all the graphs indicate? First, there are millions of salmon, halibut, and herring which live within the bioregion. Second, these species have been overfished to the point where natural populations are under severe stress. Third, the commercial fishing industry, dominated in British Columbia by only several large companies, has centralized cannery operations, stunting the economies of dozens of coastal settlements.

Under bioregional stewardship, salmon would be harvested near the stream of their origin. Essential protein would be made available at low cost in the bioregion, helping to attract and maintain a stable population. Export of value-added fish products would provide employment and fair returns of profit and local government revenue. Small canneries would be located all along the coast, underpinning the social and economic life of communities which also relied on restoration of damaged forest habitats, and sustainable extraction of trees, minerals, and crops.

Source: compiled from Argue, A. W., and M. P. Shepard, *Historical Trends In British Columbia Salmon Catch and Production: Commercial Catch 1873-1982*. Vancouver: Canada Deptartment of Fisheries and Oceans, 1985; British Columbia, Commissioner of Fisheries, *Report of the Commis-*

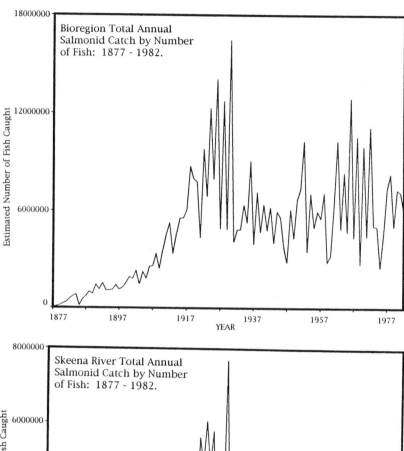

Bioregion Total Annual Salmonid Catch by Number of Fish: 1877 - 1982.

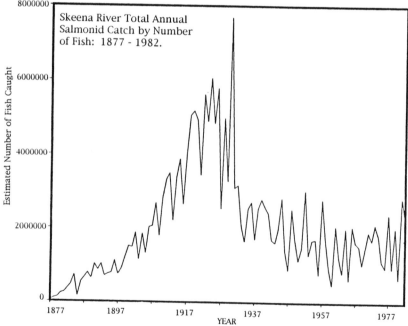

Skeena River Total Annual Salmonid Catch by Number of Fish: 1877 - 1982.

sioner of Fisheries 1902-1928. Victoria: King and Queen's Printer, 1903-1929; Canada, Department of Fisheries and Oceans, *Annual Reports 1877-1946.* Ottawa: King and Queen's Printer: 1878- 1947; Canada, Department of Fisheries and Oceans, *Annual Summary of British Columbia Catch Statistics 1969-1982.* n.p.: n.p., 1970-1983; Canada, Department of Fisheries and Oceans, *British Columbia Catch Statistics 1951-1982.* n.p: n.p., 1952-1983.

Bioregion Mining Industry Profile

Plotting the weight of minerals taken from the earth in any bioregion is a relatively simple task. For over a century, most state and provincial governments have collected production information for each mine that has been in existence. Much of this data has recently been computerized, making it available in any number of formats.

Charting mineral extraction volumes and rates in your bioregion will again layer your understanding of both how the land has been exploited, and what opportunities it holds. The identification of large companies that own mineral rights in your bioregion can also lead to investigation of their world-wide holdings, and the compilation of a profile that will indicate how they might, or might not, respect local cultures and environments. Areas of historic mining activity may be the first places to accent environmental monitoring, as past industry pollution control practices were poor.

Example: mining is another major industry in the Northwest bioregion. To accurately describe how the industry has historically operated, the following maps, tables, and graphs were created for the period between 1902 and 1983 (two only are provided for illustration):

- Bioregion mine identification key showing mine name, latitude and longitude, rivershed name, and supply settlement;
- Bioregion areas of concentrated mining activity;
- Bioregion total mineral production;
- Bioregion total mineral production by drainage basin;
- Bioregion mineral production by individual mine;
- Operating life of bioregion mines in years;
- Number of bioregion mines operating by year;
- Bioregion annual production of gold, silver, copper, lead, zinc, molybdenum, iron, and minor minerals.

The above investigation showed that a staggering volume of minerals has been consistently extracted from within the bioregion. Of 157 mines identified, the majority of production originated from only a handful of massive sites. These developments have traditionally attracted a "single-

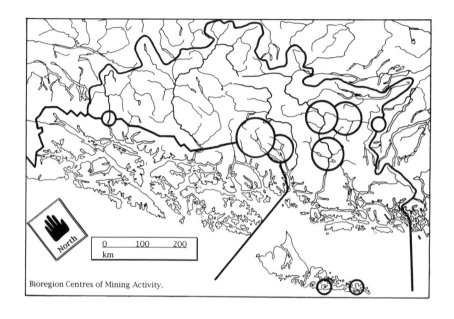

Bioregion Centres of Mining Activity.

Bioregion Total Mineral Production 1902 - 1983			
Mineral	Kilograms	Imp. Pounds	Short Tons
Gold	105,363	232,283	116
Silver	3,392,008	7,478,021	3,739
Copper	—	—	1,036,059
Lead	—	—	67,383
Zinc	—	—	101,207
Molybdenum	—	—	14,969
Iron	—	—	8,507,830
Cobalt	785	1,731	<1
Cadmium	490,520	1,081,393	541
Tungsten	1,037,540	2,287,346	1,144
Antimony	6,302	13,893	7

industry" town that is abandoned when the ore runs out.

From these observations a number of bioregional approaches to the mining industry can be proposed. First, localized workforces could be trained in small-scale mining techniques. Ore could be stockpiled and either treated by a mobile concentrator, or shipped to a smelter located in the bioregion. The bioregion government could seek full benefit of taxes generated by mineral production. Smelted ore could be fed to small, dispersed manufacturing plants configured to produce the wide range of items necessary to achieve a high degree of material self-reliance. Vigilance would be maintained to eliminate negative environmental impacts of all these activities.

Again it should be emphasized that the level of detail represented in the assessment of any industry in any bioregion should not be intimidating. Each graph or table is simply a compendium of single numbers which combine to demonstrate an extraction trend.

Source: British Columbia, Ministry of Energy, Mines, and Petroleum Resources, *Minfile*. Victoria: Queen's Printer, 1982.

Bioregion Forest Industry Profile

The volume of timber taken from forests is by far the most difficult extraction trend to chart. This difficulty arises from the sheer magnitude of the industry, reporting methodology that is not area specific, and many changes in the size of administrative areas within which cut statistics are calculated. It will take some amount of persistence, and some lucky guesses, to calculate extraction levels over a bioregion area that does not conform to forestry related administrative jurisdictions that have remained consistent over time. In this situation all you can do is your best, and not worry if the reporting areas are fractionally larger or smaller that bioregion limits.

It should be noted that in some cases the units of measure used in the forest harvest graphs were custom-made to aid their comprehension. The volumes of tree extraction are so large that three unique measures were created. First, the industry unit of harvest, the cubic meter, was translated into standard tree equivalents. This measure relates harvest to a standard size tree 50 feet long and 18 inches in diameter. Second, harvest volumes were related to the number of railroad boxcars that would be filled with wood. Third, the length of train created by the filled boxcars was charted. As with relating salmon caught to each individual living fish, the goal of creating the above measures is to communicate extraction levels in terms that clearly describe their magnitude.

Example: since the end of World War II, forestry has become the dominant industry in Northwest B.C. To accurately understand the

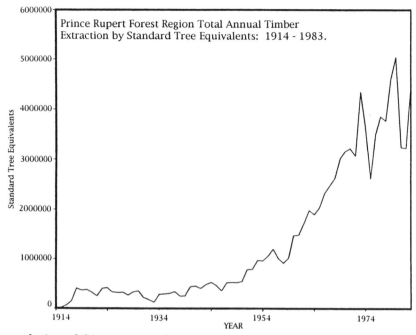

Prince Rupert Forest Region Total Annual Timber Extraction by Standard Tree Equivalents: 1914 - 1983.

evolution of this segment of the bioregion economy it was necessary to create the following tables and graphs which cover a reporting period between 1914 and 1983 (two only are provided for illustration):

- Prince Rupert Forest Region annual timber harvest 1913- 1983;
- Prince Rupert Forest Region harvest by coast and interior harvest areas;
- Prince Rupert Forest Region species comparison of total coast and interior statistical area harvests;
- Prince Rupert Forest Region annual timber harvest in standard tree equivalents;
- Prince Rupert Forest Region annual timber harvest in boxcar equivalents;
- Prince Rupert Forest Region annual timber harvest in freight train length equivalents;
- Bioregion annual pulp and paper production;
- Prince Rupert Forest Region number of operating sawmills by year;
- Prince Rupert Forest Region annual extraction by fir, cedar, spruce, hemlock, balsam, lodgepole pine, cottonwood, cypress, hardwood, and miscellaneous species.

The results of the above investigations show a forest industry that has an ever increasing appetite for "fibre." The number of sawmills in the region has sharply declined, while the remaining modern sawmills grow larger and provide less employment. Harvest levels climbed steadily for 25 years, and while still trending upward since 1975, have fluctuated wildly in various oil embargoes and recessions. By the mid-1980s, approximately five million "standard tree equivalents" were being extracted annually in the bioregion. This volume of timber would fill 115,000 boxcars, a number that if linked together would make a train nearly 950 miles long. The primary result of this pillage is that the most accessible stocks of prime tree species in the bioregion have been decimated, with accelerating pressure being put upon species with lesser commercial value.

Under bioregional stewardship, extraction rates from Northwest forests could be considerably reduced. Local governments could extend their boundaries over adjacent forests, and implement wholistic forestry regimes devised to maintain sustainable harvests. Trees that continue to be cut could be manufactured into value-added products, both for local use and for export. A major focus of production would be modular elements for energy efficient housing, furniture, and fine paper. As with the fishery and mining sectors, community economies would be supported by small, quality-oriented conversion plants, powered by

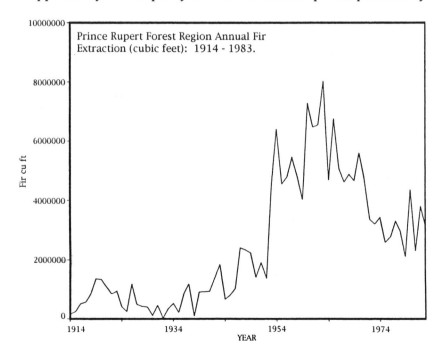

Prince Rupert Forest Region Annual Fir Extraction (cubic feet): 1914 - 1983.

locally-generated sources of electricity.

Source: British Columbia, Ministry of Forests, *Annual Reports 1914-1983*. Victoria: King and Queen's Printer, 1915-1984.

Bioregion Agricultural Industries Profile

As with the natural resources we have already discussed, it is a relatively simple task to chart the annual harvests of food crops in your bioregion. This information is commonly available from state or provincial agriculture agencies, or from university libraries.

In reviewing past and present agricultural activity it will also be useful to record the crops that were grown in different historical eras, how they were used, and how land ownership and development patterns evolved into present agricultural land uses. It would be equally important to understand the current destinations of local crops, as this may indicate the kinds of secondary food enterprises that may be located in the bioregion.

Example: agriculture harvests were not charted for the Northwest due to the minimal amount of farming which exists in the bioregion. In areas where agriculture plays an important part in the economy, the following graphs could be researched:

- Bioregion annual crop harvests by type, volume, area of cultivation;
- Number and average size of bioregion farm units by year;
- Average bioregion farm unit use of herbicides/pesticides/fertilizers by volume and by year;
- Analysis of sites that offer geothermal, or industrial waste heat, for greenhouse use;
- Etc.

The great majority of food required to feed the Northwest bioregion population could be grown internally. The most productive farmland could be fully used, and the heat available as a byproduct of manufacturing utilized for greenhouse heating. While beef production would fall, relatively low prices for salmon protein would easily fill the gap. Incentives could be provided for the organization of producer-owned cooperatives that would minimize investment, and maximize returns to growers. Family garden plots could be made available to all urban residents. A transportation energy tax on imported food products could ensure a ready market for local growers, and would supply revenue for an active permaculture extension program.

*

The economy of any bioregion is complex. To understand what engines of commerce drive the juggernaut of development in your home area requires study and patience. This level of scrutiny will not be to everyone's taste but, as already stated, the rewards for those who stick with the investigation will be many. A reinhabitant may fantasize about the cooperative utopia that could exist under a bioregional regime, but to build that utopia will require the dismantling of an existing economic system whose strength partially depends on its mystery. By understanding how major parts of the existing economy of your bioregion are structured, you will be empowered to begin their transformation.

◆

Section 4:
Mapping Local Areas

For many people, the process of evolving a bioregional perception may best start with mapping the relatively small area around the place where they live. This approach will be especially useful for people living in urban areas. To understand the intricacies of a more localized set of biocultural relationships, including those dominated by the human-built environment, the completion of an additional series of mapping exercises may be useful.

When trying to define the borders of large bioregions, the information required is at a "macro," or generalized, level. If your interest is more localized, the type of data you require is at a "micro" level that requires the use of a large scale base map to be properly represented.

To find the type of neighborhood base map you require, there are several alternatives that can be followed. First, you can simply purchase a topographic map that covers your home area. These maps are normally produced at either a one to 50,000, or one to 25,000 scale. This means that a mile on each map would respectively cover 1.27 or 2.53 inches of image. By cutting off borders with scissors, several of these maps can easily be taped together to cover the local area you wish to study.

Second, you can visit your local government office and ask to see the range of custom-made maps that have been created to cover the particular municipal, county, or regional jurisdiction within which you live. The best approach is to ask to speak to either the town planner or draftsperson. These people will know most about maps, and will usually be pleased to show off the images which they create and use.

Third, you can find the state or provincial agency that handles maps and air photos. Usually a catalogue is available of the maps which cover your area. Either color or black and white air photos can be ordered. These images are typically nine by nine inches in size, and are photographed to cover map scales between one to 10,000 and one to 25,000 (one mile equals 6.34 and 2.53 inches of image respectively). Multiple air photos can be combined into one "composite" image at the original scale, or be enlarged to any level of detail required. Maps used for neighborhood scale planning purposes should be at a scale of 400 or fewer feet to one inch of map image; larger study areas can be adequately represented at smaller scales.

Once you have chosen a base map, it is necessary to tape successive pieces of tracing paper over the original map image. Using this technique it will be possible to create any number of thematic maps representing data which interest you. These individual sheets can then be used as overlays to make any number of combined images on a light table. Alternatively, you can either purchase multiple copies of your base map, or chart all your data directly on the base map. The latter technique will create an extremely busy image which will be useful in conveying the richness of natural and human activity in your neighborhood area, but can be short on clarity.

When your base map is organized, what kinds of information should you begin to transcribe? The possibilities are endless. What follows is just a hint at the lifetime of ways that part of a bioregion can be learned:

Biophysical Environment:
- Color elevation contours;
- Chart sun paths as they change through the seasons;
- Mark the location of bird and wildlife sightings;
- Take climate readings, make a microclimate profile;
- Make a map of indigenous plant and animal species that inhabited the area before European contact;
- Chart location of creeks, streams, wetlands, and estuaries, including those which may have been paved over, captured in culverts, or landfilled;
- Show the web of green spaces that currently covers the map area, name plant associations, propose links to nearby green areas.

Human Environment:
- Identify sources of water, food, energy, waste disposal, sewage treatment;
- Identify vacant publicly owned land;
- Delineate "neighborhood village" boundaries, prepare census pro-

files;

- Locate recreation and cultural amenities in the area;
- Locate environmental hazards such as dumps, toxic waste sites, sewer outfalls, etc.;
- Locate public safety amenities, including hospitals, and fire hydrants;
- Create a map showing local trails;
- Identify the holdings of large landowners in your area;
- Chart the age and condition of infrastructure, including roads, sidewalks, street trees, etc.;
- Identify roadways which are dangerous for pedestrians or bicycles;
- Identify barriers to access by children and the physically challenged;
- Locate heritage buildings, mark their age and condition, list their current owners;
- Show any special "power spots" that are good for meditation and/or reflection;
- Show the location of local gardens and fruit trees;
- Show the location of ten locally-owned businesses most important for the community to support;
- Show areas of high crime, and persistent pedestrian conflicts with traffic;
- Identify dark areas where better lighting can be promoted;
- Show places where kids can interact with the natural environment;
- Pinpoint sources of pollution, list chemicals;
- Locate the ten largest employers in the area, list donations and other support they tithe to the community;
- Locate old land use maps and transfer to a standard format map series, highlight how the community has grown or declined over time.

The type of information which a neighborhood bioregion atlas can show is almost endless. Over a number of years, and aided by the perceptions and interest of many reinhabitants, the atlas becomes an essential repository of local fact, lore, and opinion. The obvious next step is to use the atlas to mount a persistent and informed campaign to achieve bioregional ideals at the local level. This means that a map of crime "blackspots" would be used by the community crime patrol, the map of vacant public land used to locate community gardens, and knowledge of neighborhood borders used to show where new urban village governments could be constituted. Maps should never be considered to be ends in themselves; they should be made to aid the

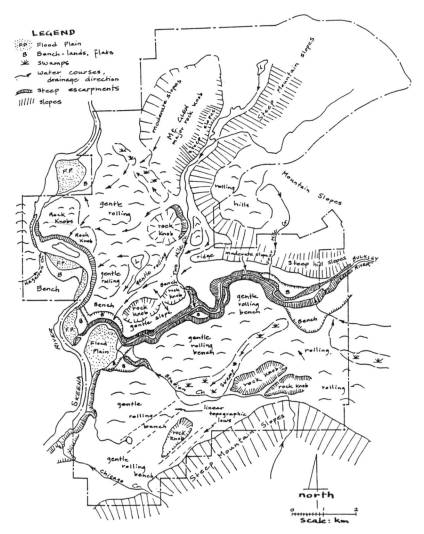

Community Sketch: Hazelton, British Columbia.

transformation to bioregional, sustainable cultures. A legacy of each successive generation in a local community would be the written and mapped knowledge it would pass on to new generations of community stewards.

◆

Section 5: Conclusion

The purpose of this bioregion mapping primer has been to introduce you to some of the many ways in which a bioregion can be identified and described. If you have persevered and completed even a portion of the exercises outlined, you will have gained a new and enduring perception of the biocultural terrain of which you are a part. What is done with your new-found knowledge and research skills is up to you. At minimum, you will have personally gained a much deeper appreciation of natural and human forces which shape your home region. Beyond personal satisfaction, you will have also created a resource that could become an invaluable teaching and bioregional advocacy tool.

In the process of trying to create a reinhabitant's atlas, you will have also thought of different ways that bioregions could be described. Tell others what you have devised. As this information is shared and continuously expanded, bioregions will be illuminated in scores of ways.

It should be clearly understood that individuals or groups working with the same information, and living in the same bioregion, may come up with borders or other findings which do not match. This is nothing to worry about. What is more important is that an effort has been made to widen perception of the social and physical territory which supports you. It is a next step to discuss the results of your exploration with others, to listen to different interpretations and work to reach a consensus of purpose.

The lasting benefit of bioregion mapping is that in many small ways you will be changed forever. In learning how to make simple images of place, your surrender to forces which abuse social justice or harm natural ecosystems will be harder to tolerate. You will have learned the language of a practical and desperately needed bioregional alternative.

Copies of the full study from which this primer is extracted — "Bioregionalism: A Territorial Approach To Governance and Development of Northwest British Columbia" — are available for CAN$40.00 plus postage from the author, c/o New Society Publishers, Canada.

6

Evolving Maps, Evolving Selves: Access to Further Resources

Doug Aberley

This volume opened with a stark appraisal of the role that mapping plays in contemporary western society. It then quickly ventured into more hopeful ground, showing how mapping can be purposefully used as a tool to visualize the connections between land and life and human culture. An appreciation of aboriginal cartography visited Micronesia, the Arctic, and the First Nations of Northwest British Columbia. The experience of contemporary grassroots organizations with conceiving and creating maps was described — a variety of effort resident in city and rural locations, using tools that range from pencils to the most sophisticated computer software. Ideas about cartographic design, thoughtful discussion of "life place" boundary definition, and the use of maps in ecological planning were introduced. Finally, a simple method for building maps as a means to identify biologically and culturally defined territories — bioregions — was demonstrated.

These explorations were organized to make the transition from a bleak status quo to the more hopeful possibilities found in the inspired mapping experience of grassroots people, and the use of a simple method for making images of already familiar home regions. It has been a great deal of material to cover in one small volume, but necessary to demonstrate the important role that mapping is playing in a wider process of social change. Before leaving you to get on with your chosen mapping tasks, there are two final insights that can be distilled from the variety of mapping thought that has been presented.

The first insight is obvious: if images of our neighborhoods, our communities, and our regions are made by others, then it is *their* future that will be imposed. But if maps are made by resident groups and individuals who have quality of life as a goal, then images of a very different nature will predominate. Locally-made maps will hang on the walls of community halls, town offices, and in school corridors. They will communicate layers of interconnected alternatives that can be implemented by persistent and courageous local action. The wisdom that this alternative vision speaks — sustainability, self-reliance, social justice — an incorruptible, decentralized power that is almost impossible to divert: the first step toward abandoning a status quo based on globalized corporate control, the commoditization of life, and institutionalized exploitation.

The second insight is that the building of local maps will have a benefit beyond the powerful promise that the finished images will contain. Although maps that show patterns of interwoven life will become a vital part of reinhabitant language, it will be the process of making the maps that will be most empowering. To build our maps, we will once again range over our territories, learning the flows of energy that offer limit and opportunity. In drawing alternative visions, we will travel far afield to see how others use renewable energy technology, operate a land trust, or resist imposed development. In sensing the history of the human occupation of our regions, we will meet cultures already rooted in the land we occupy. By evolving maps which speak our alternative, we will more importantly be evolving ourselves. We will be transformed by the active reinhabitation of place — home again in the territories that our new maps describe.

Access to Further Resources

In a society inundated with sources of information, it is often a difficult task to identify where to start when trying to learn a new skill such as mapping. The following resource list is intended to be a simple education aid, providing access to several sources for major topics touched upon in this volume. It is not an exhaustive listing, but does include many of the titles that seem to show up in the libraries of those who practice local mapping.

A note of caution, however: before you rush out and order any of these books, maps, or journals, take a look at them first at your local or regional library. It will also be useful to look at the bibliographies of the volumes suggested, and to browse for new titles that may include up-to-date information on fast changing subjects like community GIS, or new atlases. When writing to any of the local organizations listed, please send a small donation to cover postage and handling costs. Any selection. marked with a asterisk is a classic source that should be read by every aspiring reinhabitant.

History of Cartography

Detailed impressions of more than 5000 years of primarily western cartographic invention can be found in:

Bagrow, Leo, *History of Cartography*. London: C. A. Watts and Co., 1964;

Thrower, Norman J. W., *Maps and Man: An Examination of Cartography in Relation to Culture and Civilization*. Englewood Cliffs, New Jersey: Prentice-Hall, 1972;

*Harley, J. B., David Woodward (eds.), *The History of Cartography*, vol. 1. Chicago: University of Chicago Press, 1987.

Cartography

There are many books which describe the technical skills necessary to construct maps. Books by Raisz and Robinson stand out because they represent past and present standard university level teaching texts. Monmonier's book is important because it shows how maps can be used to manipulate a public that often does not understand how cartographic images are made.

Monmonier, Mark, *How To Lie With Maps*. Chicago: University of Chicago Press, 1991;

Raisz, Erwin, *General Cartography*. New York: McGraw-Hill, 1938 (*) and 1948;

Raisz, Erwin, *Principles of Cartography*. New York: McGraw-Hill, 1962. (It may be interesting to look at all three volumes to see how a celebrated cartographer evolved his description of cartography over a thirty year period.)

Robinson, Arthur, Randall Sale, Joel Morrison, *Elements of Cartography*. New York: John Wiley, 1978.

Map Availability / Access to Cartographic Resources

There are relatively few sources which give an introduction to the contemporary state of cartographic knowledge, as well as provide detailed listing of types of maps available and how they can be ordered. These books are commonly held by large libraries:

Böhme, Rolf (ed.), *Inventory Of World Topographic Mapping*, 2 volumes. London: Elsevier Applied Science Publishers, 1989 and 1991;

Makower, Joel (ed.), *The Map Catalog*. New York: Vintage Books, 1990;

Parry, R. B., C. R. Perkins, *World Mapping Today*. London: Butterworths, 1987;

*Perkins, C. R., R. B. Parry (eds.), *Information Sources in Cartography*. London: Bowker-Saur, 1990.

Retail Map Supply

Most large cities host at least one outlet that stocks a comprehensive supply of maps. If you live where maps aren't easily available, you have two choices of access. You can use various guides to seek out sources of individual types of maps, or you can write to a mail order outlet that can supply a number of different image types from one location. Several of the largest mail order operations are:

Geoscience Resources, 2990 Anthony Road, P.O. Box 2096, Burlington, North Carolina, U.S.A. 27216.

Map Link, 529 State Street, Santa Barbara, California, U.S.A. 93101.

World Wide Books and Maps, 736A Granville Street, Vancouver, British Columbia, Canada V6Z 1G3.

National Atlases

Perhaps the best way to get started with mapping is to leaf through a national atlas. Borders, climate, history, and bounty are depicted in an attempt to communicate legitimacy of the nation state. Although images in these volumes cover very large territories, and hence suffer from lack of detail, they nonetheless convey the great range of subject material that can be shown in map form.

National Atlas of Canada. Ottawa: Energy Mines and Resources Canada, 1985. (1:7,500,000);

National Atlas of the United States. Washinton DC: U.S. Deptartment of the Interior, 1970. (1:7,500,00);

Atlas Nacional del Medio Físico. Mexico: Dirección General de Geographía, 1981. (1:1,000,000).

Map Design Ideas

There are countless ways to draw maps; these books are fun sources of inspiration:

Holmes, Nigel, *Pictoral Maps*. London: The Herbert Press, 1991;

Southworth, Michael and Susan, *Maps: A Visual Survey and Design Guide*. New York: Little, Brown, 1982;

Alpha, Tan Ro, Janis Dellerman, James Morley, *Atlas of Oblique Maps: A Collection of Landform Portrayals of Selected Areas of the World*, Miscellaneous Investigations Series I-1799. Reston, Virginia: U.S. Geological Survey, 1988.

Aboriginal Mapping

The best sources of current information on aboriginal mapping are to be found in research prepared by aboriginal peoples in their hundreds of "land claim" challenges against central governments. Check local aboriginal organizations for what might be available. A sample of books which include reference to aboriginal perceptions of time and space include:

Adler, Bruno F., "Maps of Primitive Peoples," *Bulletin of the Imperial Society of Students of Natural History, Anthropology and Ethnography, at the Imperial University of Moscow*, 119.2, 1910. (Rare, in Russian.);

Brice-Bennet, Carol (ed.) *Our Footprints Are Everywhere: Inuit Land Use And Occupancy In Labrador*. Nain, Labrador: Labrador Inuit Association, 1977;

Brower, Kenneth, *A Song For Satawal*. New York: Penguin, 1984;

Brody, Hugh, *Maps and Dreams: Indians And The British Columbian Frontier*.

London: Jill Norman and Hobhouse, 1981;

Chatwin, Bruce, *The Songlines*. New York: Penguin, 1987;

Farrell, Lindsay, *Unwritten Knowledge: Case Study of the Navigators of Micronesia*. Victoria: Deakin University, 1984;

Freeman, Milton M. R. (ed.), *Inuit Land Use and Occupancy Project*, 3 volumes. Ottawa: Indian and Northern Affairs Canada/Ministry of Supply and Services, 1976;

Gladwin, Thomas, *East is a Big Bird: Navigation and Logic on Puluwat Atoll*. Cambridge, Mass.: Harvard University Press, 1970;

de Hutorowicz, H., "Maps of Primitive Peoples," *Bulletin of the American Geographical Society*, 43.9, 1911: 669-679;

Lewis, David, *We, the Navigators: The Ancient Art of Land Finding in the Pacific*. Canberra: Australian National University Press, 1972;

Lopez, Barry, *Arctic Dreams: Imagination and Desire in a Northern Landscape*. New York: Charles Scribner's Sons, 1986;

Lyons, Henry, "The Sailing Charts of the Marshall Islanders." *The Geographical Journal*. 72, 1928: 325- 328.

Mapping of North America

There are several remarkable volumes which vividly show the wonder North America has inspired in early and contemporary western cartographers. These sources are useful in that they treat Turtle Island as a whole, not just as a patchwork of dissected political entities.

Cumming, W. P., R. A. Skelton, D. B. Quinn, *The Discovery of North America*. London, Paul Eleck, 1971;

Cumming, W. P. and S. Hillier, D. B. Quinn, G. Williams, *The Exploration of North America 1630-1776*. London: Paul Elek, 1974;

Garret, Wilbur (ed.), *Atlas of North America: Space Age Portrait Of A Continent*. Washington, DC: National Geographic Society, 1985.

Cognitive Mapping

Cognitive mapping enjoys a persistent popularity as a topic of geographical research. Although these volumes all suffer a bit from specialized language, they are important references for understanding how "mental maps" play a critically important role in human life and culture.

Downs, Roger M., and David Stea, *Maps In Minds: Reflections On Cognitive Mapping*. New York: Harper and Row, 1977;

Saarinen, Thomas F., *Environmental Planning: Perception and Behavior*. Atlanta: Houghton Mifflin, 1976.

Perceptions of Place

"Place" is a word that is central to local mapping. It is often used casually, with too little explanation of the meaning with which it is invested. These books all describe variations of the concept of place:

Garreau, Joel, *Edge City: Life On The New Frontier*. New York: Doubleday, 1991;

Hall, Edward T., *The Hidden Dimension*. Garden City, New York: Doubleday,

1966;

Hiss, Tony, *The Experience of Place*. New York: Knopf, 1990;

*Tuan, Yi-Fu, *Topophilia: A Study of Environmental Perception, Attitudes, and Values*. Englewood Cliffs, New Jersey: Prentice- Hall, 1974.

Bioregionalism

Bioregionalism can provide the all-important context that makes local mapping a language of transformative change. Images of place drawn without purpose remain only images. If they are constructed to achieve some sustainable alternative to the status quo, then they become something much more powerful. Basic information on bioregionalism can be found in:

*Andruss, Van, Christopher Plant, Judith Plant, Eleanor Wright (eds.), *Home! A Bioregional Reader*. Philadelphia: New Society Publishers, 1990;

Berry, Thomas, *The Dream of the Earth*. San Francisco: Sierra Club Books, 1988;

Plant, Christopher, Judith Plant, *Turtle Talk: Voices For A Sustainable Future*, The New Catalyst Bioregional Series vol. 1. Philadelphia, PA and Gabriola Island, BC: New Society Publishers, 1990. (This volume is an introduction to bioregionalism; other volumes in the series cover aspects such as local economics, and political decentralization.)

Raise the Stakes. Subscription information from Planet Drum Foundation, P.O. Box 31251, San Francisco, CA, Shasta Bioregion, U.S.A. 94131.

*Sale, Kirkpatrick, *Dwellers in the Land: The Bioregional Vision*. Philadelphia, PA and Gabriola Island, BC: New Society Publishers, 1985.

Ecological Mapping

The following books are not just about ecological mapping. Each approaches the subject of human agency on the Earth from a different direction, using a range of ideas and techniques that assist in evolving detailed functional knowledge of balance, opportunity, and limit.

*Alexander, Christopher, Sara Ishikawa, Murray Silverstein, *A Pattern Language: Towns, Buildings, Construction*. New York: Oxford University Press, 1977;

*van Dresser, Peter, *Landscape for Humans: A Case Study of the Potentials for Ecologically Guided Development in an Uplands Region*. Albuquerque: Biotechnic Press, 1972;

Lyle, John Tillman, *Design For Human Ecosystems: Landscape, Land Use and Natural Resources*. New York: Van Nostrand Reinhold, 1985;

Marsh, William M., *Landscape Planning: Environmental Applications*. New York: John Wiley, 1991;

*McHarg, Ian L., *Design With Nature*. Garden City, New York: Doubleday, 1971;

Steiner, Frederick, *The Living Landscape: An Ecological Approach To Landscape Planning*. New York: McGraw-Hill, 1991.

Geographic Information Systems (GIS)

With hardware costs plummeting and software developers anxious to establish new customers, GIS use is spreading well beyond its traditional business, government, and academic markets. In such a rapidly changing field the best sources of information will be a mix of periodicals and reports from grassroots organizations who have actual experience with GIS attributes and pitfalls.

Burrough, P. A., *Principles of Geographic Information Systems For Land Resource Assessment*. Oxford: Clarendon Press, 1986;

Computer Graphics World. Subscription information from: PennWell Publishing Co., 1421 South Sheridan, P.O. Box 1260, Tulsa, Oklahoma, U.S.A. 74101;

ESRI Systems Inc., 380 New York Street, Redlands, CA U.S.A. 92373. (For information on one only of several popular GIS software programs.);

Geographic Information Systems support for environmental groups: an investigative study. (61 pages). Inquire regarding price and other available material to: Greater Ecosystems Alliance. P.O. Box 2813, Bellingham, WA U.S.A. 98227;

International Journal of Geographic Information Systems. Subscription information from: Taylor and Francis Limited. 4 John Street, London, U.K. WC1N 2ET;

GIS World. Subscription information from P.O. Box 8090, Fort Collins, CO. U.S.A. 80526;

Mapping Awareness and GIS Europe. Subscription information from: Miles Arnold, Grey Cottage, Cassington, Oxfordshire, U.K. OX8 1BR.

Biodiversity and "GAP" Mapping

This is another quickly evolving area of map use. Conservation activists are using GIS to: 1) identify distribution of various levels of ecological association; 2) identify remaining areas where these associations have not been damaged; and 3) show how remaining wild areas might be enlarged and linked together in a manner to protect biodiversity.

*Foreman, Dave (ed.), "The Wildlands Project: Plotting A North American Wilderness Recovery Strategy," Special Issue of *Wild Earth*. Information from: P.O. Box 5365, Tucson, AZ U.S.A. 85703;

Scott, J. Michael, et al, *GAP Analysis: A geographic approach to protection of biological diversity*, Wildlife Monograph No. 123, supplement to *The Journal of Wildlife Management*. 57.1 (Jan. 1993).

Request current information from:

British Columbia Gap Analysis Newsletter, Earthlife Canada. P.O. Box 47105, #19, 555 West 12th Ave., Vancouver, B.C. Canada V5Z 4L6.

Mr. Michael Jennings, Idaho Cooperative Fish and Wildlife Research Unit. Deptartment of Fish and Wildlife Resources, College of Forestry, Wildlife, and Range Sciences, University of Idaho, Moscow, ID U.S.A. 83843.

Map Rap, P.O. Box 151, Leggett, CA U.S.A. 95455.

Inspirational Sources

If you review a large number of maps and associated written sources for local or bioregional mapping research, there are occasionally those that are especially inspiring. Some may be special for their wealth of information, others for their beauty, original idea, or format. Others are immediately recognizable as the work of a gifted craftsperson who builds images of land and culture with uncommon skill. The following list of personal favorites does not repeat citings already made in the book, and provides only a small sample of sources that are worth the time it takes to seek them out.

Annals of the Association of American Geographers. Geography is a broad discipline whose practitioners refuse to settle on any reductionist notion of exactly what they should study. Because of this ambiguity, articles in journals like *Annals* cover an incredible amount of useful territory. See Volume 82 (September 1992) for a selection of thought around the topic of North America before and after 1492. Subscription information from: Blackwell Publishers, Journals Department, 3 Cambridge Center, Cambridge, MA U.S.A. 02142.

Canadian Cartographics. Over the last twenty years independent cartographer Lou Skoda has been contracted to create an extraordinary number of beautiful and important images of British Columbia. *Biogeoclimatic Zones of British Columbia, Kitimat-Stikine Regional District Regional Resource Inventory, Georgia Strait Urban Region, Energy Resources of British Columbia, Canada's Pacific Coast Fisheries Resources and Competing Resource Uses* and *Water Use: Strait of Georgia and Puget Sound* are all immediately recognizable as his careful work. These images reveal complex patterns of ecological association and human land use in a manner that both educates and inspires. For information on map availability and price contact: Canadian Cartographics, Unit 106, 3680 Bonneville Place, Burnaby, British Columbia, Canada V3N 4T5.

Cruikshank, Julie, *Reading Voices: Oral and Written Interpretations of the Yukon's Past.* Vancouver: Douglas & McIntyre, 1991. Although not specifically about mapping, this book is definitely about "place." From the experience of aboriginal elders, an image of Yukon land and culture emerges in many layers of perception. This is the type of book that reinhabitants of every bioregion could use to teach "home."

The GeoSphere Project. It is Tom Van Sant's mission to build "from space" images of the planet through the use of color mosaic satellite imagery. Thousands of digitized images taken by Advanced Very High Resolution Radiometer satellites are processed so that they seam together in remarkable cloudless views. In addition to producing a growing variety of striking maps, the GeoSphere Project is working on globes seven to sixteen feet in diameter which will be the focus of global environmental monitoring efforts. For information write: The GeoSphere Project, P.O. Box 421, Clarkson P.O., Mississauga, ON Canada L5T 3Y2.

Kahrl, William L. (ed.), *The California Water Atlas.* Sacramento: The Governor's Office of Planning and Research, 1979. In this compendium of impressive images, water distribution in California is shown in all its natural and human adapted patterns. Created under the auspices of then-Governor Jerry Brown, it was a successful attempt to show an important natural element in its totality, not just as it existed in isolated pieces. The impact of the atlas is communication of great despair that a land once so invested with natural capital has been so quickly plundered and "improved."

Erwin Raisz Landform Maps. Erwin Raisz was a legendary cartographer expert at creating intricately drawn small-scale maps which clearly depicted landscape from a bird's eye perspective (see cover). These "morphographic" images used 40 standard pictoral symbols to depict variations of landform and human land use in a manner extremely recognizable to the human eye. Until the advent of satellite imaging and computer assisted mapping, Raisz maps were the only interpretation of physiographic patterns as they ranged over large areas of the planet. His classic map *Landforms of the United States* remains available through the Raisz family. For current pricing, send a stamped self-addressed envelope to Erwin Raisz Landform Maps, P.O. Box 2254, Jamaica Plain, MA, U.S.A. 02130.

Raven Maps and Images. Raven produces maps of North America that blend the artistry of Raisz with use of state-of-the-art cartographic technology. This skill has most recently been demonstrated in their production of two small-scale maps of the coterminous United States. Using hypsometrically-tinted digital relief images these maps take your breath away: they are big, shaded for maximum legibility, and enforce the most difficult cartographic maxim of all — "simple is best." For a catalogue listing these and many other images write: Raven Maps and Images, 34 North Central, Medford, OR U.S.A. 97501.

Selkrigg, Lydia (ed.), *Alaska Regional Profiles: Southeast, Alaska.* Fairbanks: University of Alaska Arctic Environmental Information and Data Center, 1977. This is a prototype bioregional atlas, full of maps, drawings, and a hundred visual lessons that demonstrate the immutable connectedness of land, water, life, and culture. With windfall oil money, similar atlases were made for each region of Alaska. They are very rare, and cherished by those lucky enough to leaf through pages that almost smell of bear breath, exude the feel of temperate rainforest fog, and sound of glacial melt.

Suttles, Cameron, *Native Languages of the North Pacific Coast of North America,* map. Portland: Suttles, 1978. Although the purpose of this one foot by three feet map is to show spatial distribution of aboriginal languages, the base map this information is drawn upon is what makes this image special. From a vantage point in the Pacific Ocean you look on a wild coast stretching from San Francisco to Kodiac Island. In the top corners, curved mountain horizons are silhouetted against a blue night sky. As with Raisz maps, the slightly disorienting result is a mix of vertical and oblique imagery that conveys a powerful perception of distance and space.

Temple University, University of Pittsburgh, The Pennsylvania State University, *The Atlas of Pennsylvania.* Philadelphia: Temple University Press, 1989. In 286 pages anyone lucky enough to see this atlas is taken on the equivalent of a white water raft trip through the Grand Canyon of Contemporary Cartographic Expression. Information relating to Pennsylvania land and resources, history, human patterns, economic activity, and urban development is shown in such creative graphic variety that it's easy to forget to absorb the information. This volume could be looked at for years, each view bringing pleasant new understanding. A classic.

*

Descriptions of the experience that individuals or groups are having with local mapping will be gratefully received. Please send them to Doug Aberley, c/o New Society Publishers, P.O. Box 189, Gabriola Island, BC, Canada V0R 1X0.